Pink Flamingo

Regaining our Purpose in a Plastic World

Travis Avila

To Bubba and the Bean ~ Spend your years on the foundation.

Contents

PART I

THE KINGDOM

Introduction

I was at a dinner party with some friends a few years back. It was your typical, run-of-the-mill, Sunday afternoon get together. The kids were playing outside while the grown-ups stood around the kitchen making small talk. This was also our opportunity to cram as much food into our mouths as we possibly could while the littles were distracted with friends and toys, completely destroying the house. (This is the eternal parenting struggle—you can have happy kids or you can have a clean house, but you cannot have both.)

As we were updating one another on our lives—whose kids were in which sports, and which parent was actually more tired—something occurred to me. My wife and I were the only Christians in the room; the rest were atheists or agnostics. But as I listened to these friends of mine talk about what they were involved with, I started feeling *very* guilty. One friend was using the resources from his small business to help people in need and sponsoring local youth sports programs on the side. Another friend was volunteering at her kid's school. Another was serving meals at a homeless shelter. My friends weren't bragging or being pretentious; they were just excited about sharing what was going on in their lives. I could hear the passion in their voices as they spoke about the activities they were involved with. That's when it dawned on me—my non-Christian friends are better Christians than I am!

These friends are more patient, kind, loving, and generous than I am. They are constantly looking for ways to help people. *It's disgusting!* But seriously, have you ever found yourself in a similar situation? You're looking for reasons to "hate" them, as you might with an athlete or musician or someone at your job who is just *too* good at what they do to be real. It's humiliating and makes you ask yourself a bunch of really tough questions. For me, the biggest question—and the one that's been haunting me for years since that dinner party—is, what makes Christians different from everyone else? And more importantly, how do we live in light of that difference?

The Bible says we are a chosen people, royal priests, a holy nation (1 Pet. 2:9). But most days, I just feel tired. So, what gives? How do we align what the Bible says is true about us with our daily experiences? I believe these are critical questions for our time because whether it ever gets said in the news or not, this much is true: it's your risk-taking for the kingdom of God, empowered by the Holy Spirit, displayed in your communities, that the world is waiting to see.

My hope is that I can help answer those questions and provide some encouragement along the way to help you rediscover the purpose for which you were created.

Chapter 1: Flannel Board Theology

When I was a kid, Sunday mornings meant only one thing: Sunday school. Walking through the church doors every week, I was hit immediately by the familiar musty smell of furniture polish and old lady perfume. I would walk into the Sunday school room, plop my children's picture Bible on the white folding table, put my head down, hunch my shoulders over, and fight sleep as our Sunday school teachers taught us that week's bible story. Growing up in the church was both a blessing and a curse, especially as it related to theology and my understanding of the kingdom of God.

As a child, I learned about biblical stories on flannel boards. If you grew up in the church throughout the 80s and 90s, you remember them, too. They were literal boards covered with flannel fabric that cutout characters, and their background scenes, could be temporarily "stuck" to and moved around the board as the story was told. I learned about the "heroes of the faith" on these flannel boards and was introduced to two-dimensional Jesus at a young age.

The problem was, biblical stories are *not* kids' stories—especially the Old Testament stories of Israel's history—but rather narratives of deeply flawed humans struggling to keep their covenant with a God bent on rescuing them from themselves. When many of us were learning these stories as children, the scandal was intentionally removed from the narrative. We heard about David fighting Goliath, but didn't hear much about him sleeping with another man's wife—and then having that man put to death. Or Moses, who helped free his people and led them to a promised land that he couldn't inhabit himself because of his disobedience. It's these *scandals*, however, that give the whole biblical story its weightiness and connects it to our own stories because the narrative hasn't changed much over the years, has it? You and I still share the biblical characters' compromised values and commitment to the Lord.

For better or worse, this two-dimensional, flannel board theology has crept into our modern thinking, especially in Western Christian culture. Many of us have been living our lives based upon a diluted theology that offers no hope for our world because it is so disconnected from the actual story happening around us. I know that's a bold statement, but I've seen it firsthand. I've lived it myself. We've made Christianity about not smoking or drinking or cussing. We've made it about being "nice people." Certainly, there is a place for that, but no kingdom was ever taken by asking nicely.

In Matthew 28, Jesus says, *(my paraphrase)*, "Listen guys...I went into hell and took the keys from Satan. I've got the power and authority of heaven, and I'm entrusting it to you, so that you can make disciples of all nations, teaching them to do what I've done and then some."[1] Obviously, I'm taking some liberties with the language here, but I wonder if this is close to the tone Jesus might have used. And what was He asking His disciples—*us*—to do?

In the fourth chapter of Luke, Jesus actually tells us why He came:

> "The Spirit of the Lord is upon me, for he has anointed me to bring Good News to the poor. He has sent me to proclaim that captives will be released, that the blind will see, that the oppressed will be set free, and that the time of the Lord's favor has come."[2]

We are called to do the same, to lay hold of a new kingdom. I believe the evidence of this new kingdom is that the captives are released, the blind see, and the oppressed are set free. And I believe this is both spiritual and literal. The beautiful thing is that God's plan all along was to allow us to partner with Him to see this kingdom come to earth. This is our mission. Jesus came as a prototype of how we should live, then He empowered us by His Spirit to do the same. What an amazing privilege!

But it won't come easy.

> And from the days of John the Baptist until
> now the kingdom of heaven suffers violence,
> and the violent take it by force.
> (Matt. 11:12 NKJV)

In the original language, this passage doesn't so much refer to physical violence as it does an intensity of will. It might be alternatively translated as,

> And from the days of John the Baptist until
> now, the kingdom of heaven is seized by
> forceful advances, and those who are fired
> up, in eager pursuit, seize the kingdom by
> force.

This latter interpretation shows a picture of taking the kingdom of heaven through an open display of force. It's the idea that we decisively, like an armed robber, snatch up spiritual territory from "the god of this age,"[3] and claim that territory for the kingdom of heaven. And where the kingdom is, there is freedom for those bound and broken.

I don't know about you, but I'm not content with living a nice, safe life. Not anymore. Author C.S. Lewis said,

> If you read history you will find that the Christians who did most for the present world were precisely those who thought most of the next. It is since Christians have largely ceased to think of the other world that they have become so ineffective in this.[4]

We must refocus our efforts on bringing the kingdom of God to earth. So many of us settle for simply "getting through the day." Our priority often seems to hinge on making enough money to pay for the Netflix series we want to binge watch when we get home from work. But that way of life just isn't working.

According to the 2018 Nielsen report, American adults spend over 11 hours per day on some kind of electronic device.[5] *Eleven hours per day!* In a 2013 Gallup poll, it was found that on average, Americans sleep 6.8 hours per night,[6] which leaves 17.2 hours left in their day. If 6.8 hours are spent sleeping, and 11 hours of the remaining 17.2 hours are spent on devices, that leaves only 6.2 hours per day for other stuff like...you know....work, family, eating, fun. This is an issue generations past didn't have to deal with.

We live our lives 140 characters at a time, curating our imperfect worlds in an attempt to impress "friends" we don't see in real life and create false intimacy. It's not that those things are necessarily bad, it's that they're hollow. *Aren't you tired of it?* Don't you long for more than just getting through the day? Aren't we all dying for something real? Fortunately for us, God offers us a new way of living. But it's going to require us to take Jesus at His word, and it's going to require risk.

When was the last time you were able to say, "I trusted God for something only God could do, and He came through!" I want to see the kingdom of God come to earth because I see too many people around me who are bound and broken, living in a false narrative, struggling with identity, value, and purpose. It's our privilege and responsibility to tell them about a God who loves them and gave Himself for them—a God who believes in them and made them in His image.

Anxiety, depression, and suicide are at unprecedented levels, especially in the West. Our culture is producing people crippled with disorders. Did you know that anxiety affects 18% of American adults and 25% of children between 13-18 years old?[7] In 2016, there were twice as many suicides as homicides.[8] Suicide is the second

leading cause of death for people ages 10-34.[9] But in the

twelfth chapter of Romans, God offers us a new way to be

human:

> Don't copy the behavior and customs of this
>
> world, but let God transform you into a new
>
> person by changing the way you think. Then
>
> you will learn to know God's will for you, which
>
> is good and pleasing and perfect.[10]

Your risk-taking for the kingdom of God, empowered by the

Holy Spirit, displayed in your communities is what the world

is waiting to see. Our culture is literally dying for a better

way.

But I think so many of us Christians get caught up in the

day-to-day routine of life, and we forget—or have never

actually discovered—the reason we were born again! And

it's not simply to be "nice" people, or "good" parents, or "useful" employees. No, you were wonderfully made in the image of God to do something only you can do, to be a part of displaying the kingdom of God here on earth as only you can do it. My hope is that you would believe deep down in your gut that you are chosen, that you were made to lead like the royalty you are, and that you carry a priestly calling to redeem and restore the brokenness around you.

My hope is that you would make a dramatic decision to take Jesus at His word and see what He does with your life!

But I'm getting ahead of myself. First, let me tell you about Don Featherstone.

Chapter 2: Phoenicopteris Ruber Plasticus

In 1957, the United States was still recovering from World War II, which had ended 12 years earlier. The American economy was stronger than ever, and Americans were hopeful about the future. The United States' gross national product—a measure of all goods and services produced in the United States—jumped 50% from 1950 to 1960,[1] and more and more Americans now considered themselves part of the middle class. As the economy grew, so did families. These larger families were a result of the post-war baby boom, and many Americans were looking to move out of the inner city to find larger, more affordable housing. Given the scarcity of materials and manpower shortly after the war, the need for easily produced, affordable housing became paramount.

Levitt and Sons, Inc. were builders in New York who took on the challenge, building the first truly mass-produced housing development between 1947 and 1951. It was known as "Levittown," and is widely regarded as the archetype for post-war suburbs throughout the country.[2] This was a new day in American history, and things were looking up. New highways were being built to create access to these new suburbs, shopping centers were built to sustain them, and gas was $0.24/gallon. Yogi Berra and Jackie Robinson were playing baseball, and televisions were being added to almost every home so families could watch *Howdy Doody* together. This was the American dream.

While these homes met the needs of returning veterans and their families by providing a low-cost housing option, they all looked the same. There was no differentiation from home to home, which were 750-square-foot ranch style homes with two trees planted in the front yard. It was the same pattern on every street for as far as the eye could see. At this point, only one in three women were in the labor force.[3] Most were working in the home as housewives, and these women wanted some way of distinguishing their homes against the monotony of the American suburb.

Enter Don Featherstone. In 1957, Don was offered a job at Union Products, a Massachusetts-based plastics company. Before 1957, Union Products made only two-dimensional lawn ornaments. Looking to expand their business, they hired the twenty-one-year-old sculptor (a recent graduate of the Worcester Art Museum's art school) to design three-dimensional animals using—then revolutionary—injection-mold technology.

Featherstone's first attempt for Union Products was a three-dimensional plastic duck. But for his second product, Featherstone took to National Geographic for inspiration. Drawn to the vibrancy of color found in tropical wildlife, he designed the iconic plastic pink flamingo we've all seen in front yards across the country, even to this day.

"You had to mark your house somehow," Featherstone said. "A woman could pick up a flamingo at the store and come home with a piece of tropical elegance under her arm to change her humdrum house." These three-foot flamingos sold for $2.76/pair in the Sears catalog in 1958, and since then, an estimated 20 million have been purchased.

Featherstone cheekily named his creation, "*phoenicopteris ruber plasticus*." It's funny because the actual scientific name for the flamingo is *phoenicopterus ruber*. (Get it? Featherstone's flamingo was plastic....*plasticus*....okay, moving on.)

While the plastic flamingo started out as a real solution to a real problem, somewhere along the line it took on a different meaning. No one is quite sure when the switch flipped on the plastic flamingo, turning it into a cheesy lawn ornament. It likely happened over decades, but many attribute the shift to the 1972 John Waters film, *Pink*

Flamingos, which by its own definition was "an exercise in poor taste." But the truth is, no one knows for sure when the plastic flamingos went from tasteful to tacky.

But this book isn't about the plastic pink flamingo, or the film for that matter. Hopefully, you knew that going in. If you are a fan of John Waters and bought this book thinking it was a documentary, all I can say is, *Buckle up. It's gonna get weird for you.*

What I want to see more than anything is what God will do with a generation that simply takes Him at His word. You see, the plastic pink flamingo didn't lose its value until it lost its purpose.

In 1 Peter it tells us, "...you are a chosen people. You are royal priests, a holy nation, God's very own possession. As a result, you can show others the goodness of God, for he called you out of the darkness into his wonderful light."[4]

Who doesn't want to be a part of that?! A royal priesthood, partnering with God in His kingdom rule. Kind of reminds us of the Garden of Eden, right? But somewhere along the way, like Featherstone's pink flamingo, Christians went from tasteful to tacky. We lost our purpose. We were created to be holy, set apart...different. We were created to be a real solution to a real problem. In a world that's buying into a narrative that says you aren't valuable unless you have this product or look this way or have a certain amount of social media followers, we get to show people the beauty of themselves. We can declare that they were created in the image of God to bring unique and individual beauty, creativity, and purpose to His good world.

For all its benefits, social media is reshaping the way we view and value ourselves and the people around us. Don't you think it's interesting we call social media content our "feed?" We're like cattle, grazing on FOMO and body shaming. But whether it's social media, unhealthy relationships, destructive internal dialogue, or any other story we hear, we must be careful not to let this content shift the narrative we live into and degrade the human image and purpose in our world.

Believe me when I say, you were born to reign. You were made to differentiate—to be salt and light. You were made to restore and redeem in ways that only you can. Sadly, for many of us, we've been left out on the lawn too long. We've faded. We've become....plastic.

In many circles, Christianity has become a cliché, lacking any unique identifier outside of the social norm. Let me ask you this: do your friends think of you and your church community as "a chosen people or a royal priesthood?" Granted, they probably don't use those words, but I'd guess many people who don't follow Jesus think that those who do are at best, nice people who go to church on the weekend. Or worse, they believe Jesus followers are people who don't actually live the way this Jesus guy they follow says they should.

My pastor has a question that he says haunts him. It's a question he reminds us of often: "If we were to close our doors tomorrow, who, besides the people who go to this church, would even care?" It's a powerful question that keeps our church on our toes and conscious of the community around us for whom we are called to be a blessing.

So, how do we Christians rediscover the purpose for which we were created, and how do we live in light of that distinction?

Chapter 3: The Calling

Cory and Lauren are friends of mine who are hyper-focused on their purposes. Both are creatives and entrepreneurs. While they have a very diverse portfolio of projects they've worked on, the common theme is to make people feel loved. Cory and Lauren believe that God made humanity with intrinsic value and should be treated as image bearers of God. Recently, along with some other friends, they opened a wine and beer garden called "Bodega" in Los Alamos, California—a sleepy little town with a big heart on the northern end of Santa Barbara wine country. You won't find Bibles on the tables or worship music playing over the outdoor speakers, but make no mistake, this place is church. With every greeting spoken, seat offered, and glass poured, Cory and Lauren give people a space to feel valued. But Bodega was a risk. Opening it took a lot of planning, time, and money—and there was a chance it wouldn't work. But the potential of what could be outweighed the anxiety of the risk.

Cory and Lauren also started an apparel company called "LUVD," which literally clothes people in the message that they are loved. It's not a Christian company, per se....*or is it?* It's just a clothing company....*or is it?* We tend to think of some vocations as sacred and the rest as secular. But the truth is, whether you're a full-time pastor, schoolteacher, plumber, bartender, civil engineer, doctor, stay-at-home mom, blogger, or salesperson, *any* vocation can be sacred when it is co-opted by the kingdom of God. I can't tell you how many people have told me, "well, I'm *just* a...." whatever, fill-in-the-blank. But you're never *just* anything when you're doing it for the kingdom. No matter what you find yourself doing, remember it's your risk-taking for the kingdom of God, empowered by the Holy Spirit, displayed in your communities, that the world is waiting to see!

So, let's talk about what I mean by "risk-taking," because I don't mean doing something dangerous or irresponsible for the sake of some reward. What I mean by *risk* is, obedience to God in the face of opposition. I'd like to tell you more about my pastor.

David had been pastoring a multi-campus church in Michigan for four years. Things were going great. He was not looking for a change, nor was there any reasonable purpose for making a change. The church was growing, he was working with his best friends, some of which he had gone to college with and afterward, had raised kids together. As far as pastoring goes, he was living the dream. But then one day he got a call from a church in California. Their pastor had passed away from cancer a year before, and they were looking for someone to lead their church. This was the easiest decision David had ever made.

"Thanks for the consideration, but no," he said.

I mean, there was no way God was calling David to take a risk, right? Why would God move him from where he was? Things were really good. They had community. They were comfortable.

The problem was, David admittedly hadn't sought God on the decision. He just looked around at his circumstances and put two and two together. After the phone call with the church in California, David began to feel what he describes as "an internal prompting," reminding him there had been times in his life where God had called him out of his comfort zone. These times had led to growth and learning that wouldn't have been possible had he not obeyed God.

This internal prompting led David to seek God on the decision. There's something called the "Wesleyan Quadrilateral"[1] that David had used previously when trying to discern whether something might be God ordained or not. John Wesley, an 18th century theologian, used four sources for theological development: scripture, tradition, reason, and experience. David went down the list. Is this type of calling something God did with people in scripture? Yes, God consistently called biblical characters into the uncomfortable and unordinary in order to establish His purpose in the world. *Check.* Next, is there traditional evidence of God working in this way. David began asking around and realized that yes, these types of risks for the kingdom of God weren't that uncommon traditionally, even within his own community. *Check.* Next, is this reasonable? Well, maybe not based on human reason, but it wasn't totally bonkers, so....*check.* Lastly, is this how God had taught him before in his past experience. Yes. *Checkmate.*

David had followed the internal prompting by seeking God, but now what? Now that he knew this could possibly be God asking him to take a risk, how would he know for sure? Well, he wouldn't. But David began walking in the direction of the prompting. This is often how God works. He'll ask you to pursue external movement to follow an internal prompting. For David, this external movement looked like creating a laundry list of needs and requests that would need to be met in order for this to work out practically— things like schools and housing and finances.

Now, for David, this didn't feel like he was testing God. Rather, it was a step of pure desperation. He didn't want to do something that God wasn't a part of, so he needed to know that, with so much on the line, God was orchestrating all of it. Little did David know at the time, God was doing exactly that. One by one, these very specific requests and needs started coming into alignment. The California church called back to ask again after David had already said no once. Housing and schools were taken care of, David and his family came out for an incognito visit that went well, and everything continued to fall into alignment, sometimes even before they mentioned the need.

After their visit, David and his wife, Dana, just had to look at each other and shake their heads in amazement. Outside of an audible voice from God, this was as close as it was going to get. They told each other, "we can go kicking and screaming, or we can go willingly, but we're going."

Next thing they know, they're moving their four kids across the country to a church in a small town on the Central Coast of California. I wish I could tell you things got easier after that, but it didn't. Things got more difficult. But David and Dana could look back at the prompting and how, as they walked in the direction of that prompting, God took down every roadblock standing in their way—even those they tried to build themselves! This gave them confidence that, even though it was difficult, God was with them.

Another thing about taking a risk for the kingdom of God is that it has a domino effect. Housing was a major issue for David and Dana. Housing on the Central Coast is completely bananas. And by bananas, I mean *expensive*! Well, there was a couple in our church that, for the year prior to David and his family coming out, had felt God calling them to downsize. They were living in a large home, and their kids had grown and left the house. It was now more than they needed. When they heard about this new pastor and his family coming out, they jumped on it immediately, offered up their home for rent at a very reasonable price, and moved into a small apartment across town. You see, when we follow God's call, it gives others the opportunity and courage to do the same! Who knows what would have happened if any one of the people in David's story wouldn't have taken the risk to obey God and walk in the direction of His prompting?

I asked David on his first trip out, why he was even considering this move that didn't make much sense on paper. He said, "I want my kids to see their dad do something difficult for the kingdom because God asked him to." As a father myself, this cued *all* the tears.

David's story isn't about some super-spiritual pastor doing super-spiritual pastor stuff. It's the story of an ordinary man wrestling with how to live differently as one who is set apart. God didn't give David the whole playbook. He gave David a prompting—a general direction—and asked David to start taking steps in that direction. And it's the same with all of us, no matter our vocation. While I can't tell you what God has made you to do, or what your calling is, I would argue that there are three foundational practices we must live by in order to rediscover the purpose for which we were created:

1. We must be submitted to the lordship of Jesus.

2. We must be empowered by the Holy Spirit.

3. We must be engaged in our local community.

We'll explore each of these in detail, but the cool thing is that what God does with our lives when we live by these practices is unique to each of us. I've got different passions and have been asked to do different things than you have. The beautiful thing about the body of Christ is that we need each other operating in our unique giftings for this whole thing to work as it was intended.

Many of you reading this may have no idea what it is you are supposed to do with your life. That's okay! We'll talk about all of that later. My hope is that by the end of this book, you'll have a clearer picture of what that is. But you won't know unless you ask. Take time while reading to ask the Holy Spirit what that is specifically. This is where the internal promptings meet the external movement. We all have hunches about who God has made us to be and what we might want to do with our lives. I would encourage you to also take some personality tests like Myers-Briggs, StrengthsFinder and Enneagram to help you hone in on those hunches. More than taking the test though, read about the different types and see what resonates with you. For example, I'm an introvert who's top strengths are ideation, connectedness, and strategy. I'm a creative, who is able to understand and relate to different viewpoints, and am driven to achieve. Writing, speaking, playing music, and communication in general really fires me up because I'm able to connect people to ideas.

See how God has wired you through some of these assessments. Also, ask the people closest to you what they see in you. Chances are, they might know you better than you know yourself—and are usually willing to tell you the great (and not so great) things about yourself if you ask them. Then pray that God would open up doors for you to start operating in your areas of strength. You might be doing some of it already without even knowing it.

For about 12 years, I was working in business, which didn't excite me all that much, until I began moving into sales and marketing, because I was able to be creative and share ideas. Slowly and steadily, as I asked God for more opportunities and walked in the direction of the promptings He was giving me, I began to get to know

myself better. As that happened, I did more of the things

that made me feel alive and influenced my situation for

the kingdom. Looking back, I can see that my time in

business was God allowing me to hone my craft. It wasn't

the waste of time it felt like in the moment. It was both a

time of purpose for that season as well as preparing me

for the next. We just need to have spiritual eyes to see our

current circumstances through faith lenses.

God made you unique with a different set of experiences,

strengths, and skills than anyone else. And He did if for a

reason. Only you can do what you can do! And we come

alive and are able to be most effective for the kingdom of

God and people around us when we're operating in those

areas where God has given us grace.

The Bible says, God formed our innermost parts—that He

knit us together in our mother's wombs.[2] I believe that

when doing that, He not only knit our bodies together, He knit our minds, our passions, and our strengths together. I'm not trying to limit us by saying that our passions and strengths are set and immovable from birth. Of course, we can learn and grow. I'm just saying that no matter how much I try, you'll never want me working on your car. I just wasn't born with an innate mechanical sense. But writing and speaking come very naturally to me.

For many of us, most of our lives are focused on figuring out who we are and what we are supposed to do with our lives. Even my dad, who is sixty years old, is wondering what he wants to do when he grows up! He got a job right out of high school and over the next forty years, built a very good life for himself and our family. But he put some passions aside along the way and is now trying to figure out how to breathe new life into them as he approaches the "retirement" stage of his life—which is an odd thing to call it because he is incapable of slowing down. He can't *not* do something—so it's actually just a question of *what's next?*

It's never too late to rediscover your purpose. God is never done with you! But we have to do the hard work of figuring ourselves out. Between asking the Holy Spirit for direction, utilizing some widely-available practical tools, and asking those around you whom you know and trust, you can get a pretty good handle on who God has made you to be and how He has uniquely gifted you. I was 35 years old before I could tell you what my giftings were in any way that made practical sense. Some of you are still searching for that answer, and some haven't begun the hunt. But God is kind and very patient with our journey. He uses the wandering to sharpen our focus. So, don't lose heart if you haven't figured it out yet. God isn't done with you! But the first step in rediscovering the purpose for which we were created is to answer a question of lordship. We get things backwards when we begin with "what should I do with my life?" instead of "whose am I?" The short answer is...

You're a slave.

Chapter 4: Slaves to Righteousness

The apostle Paul identifies himself as a slave:

> This letter is from Paul, a slave of Christ Jesus,
>
> chosen by God to be an apostle...[1]

It's interesting to see the order in which he introduces himself. First, his identity as a slave of Jesus, then his calling as an apostle. Paul understood that everything begins with lordship. You may be saying to yourself, *Wait a minute...we're free from sin. How can we still be slaves?* You're right...in part.

Yes, we're free from sin and the punishment for that sin, which is death. But we're still slaves, no doubt about it.

> Now you are free from your slavery to sin, and
>
> you have become slaves to righteous living.[2]

We're all being shaped. The question is, who or what is shaping us, and what are we becoming? Often, even good things can make bad masters when we give them power over our lives.

How are you being shaped?

Are you continually being pulled away from your family by a job that has become a bad master? Does your social media status dictate your significance? Have you given money a more prominent role in your life than it deserves?

Money, power, relationships, career, sex—these are the bad masters that get the most press. But I believe there are more subtle, possibly more subversive, "good things gone bad" that can shape us in ways that pull us back into slavery: comfort, influence, convenience, tradition—even

Christianity itself. You might remember the stories of the Pharisees in the Bible. These were the spiritual leaders of their day; they knew the scriptures backwards and forwards. They were experts on the law which was given to Moses, and the law was good. But somewhere along the way, the Pharisees put the law above the One who gave the law. In the Gospel of Matthew, Jesus criticized the Pharisees big time for this, telling them:

> "What sorrow awaits you teachers of religious law and you Pharisees. Hypocrites! For you cross land and sea to make one convert, and then you turn that person into twice the child of hell you yourselves are!"[3]

It would seem as if Jesus cares very much about the good things that can shape us in bad ways if we allow them to. Again, we are continually being shaped. The only choice we have is over *what* is shaping us. Are there good things that are creating bad habits in your life that you need to take back control over? Are you watching too much TV? Are you drinking just a little bit more than you ought to, or putting sleep and social media ahead of time with the Lord? Are you spending just a little more time in the office than you should because your wife and two kids are at home, and they've been fighting all day, and you don't want to go home to that mess because it's much more peaceful at work, but your wife needs you home because she still needs to go to Trader Joes for bread and wants to meet up with a girlfriend after the kids are in bed? (Asking for a friend.) In chapter 5 of Galatians, Paul reminds the church that Christ died to set us free, so let's make sure we *stay* free!

See, as Christians, we aren't bound by the desires of our sinful nature anymore. We've been adopted as sons and daughters into a new kingdom. In the kingdom of God though, we enslave ourselves to God—and with that kind of enslavement comes joy, peace, and the power of the Spirit. It's the kind of life that only comes through death. The kind of surrender that brings freedom. You see, God, in His great mercy, has replaced the bondage of chains with the seal of his Spirit.

Chains restrict, so God broke them once and for all.[4] But make no mistake—you are not your own:

> Do you not know that your bodies are
> temples of the Holy Spirit, who is in you, whom
> you have received from God? You are not
> your own; you were bought at a price.
> Therefore honor God with your bodies.[5]

It's a profound mystery, this new kingdom. But I'm telling you now, when we begin to take God at His word, when we begin to walk in obedience to the Spirit, we will experience stories of biblical proportions.

Advancing the kingdom won't come comfortably. I said earlier that no kingdom was ever taken by asking nicely. It's also true that this advancement of the kingdom through binding up the brokenhearted, proclaiming freedom for the captives, releasing the prisoners from darkness, and making disciples won't come without cost. I suspect that so many of us haven't experienced the kind of Christianity we read about—and that we long for so much—because we haven't surrendered to the lordship of Christ in our lives. We haven't said, like Jesus said to the Father, "not my will, but yours be done."

Of course, we have to remember the context in which Jesus said those words. The Father's will was that Jesus would go to the cross. Jesus said, "Father, if You are willing, take this cup from me; yet not my will, but yours be done."[6] Accepting the lordship of Christ can often mean accepting risk. Sometimes the voice of the Spirit is asking us to take chances and get out of our comfort zone, but we dismiss the voice because it's asking us for more than we're comfortable giving.

I've got a friend named Lindsay. Her parents moved to Ukraine as missionaries when she was five years old. After 18 years in Ukraine, Lindsay moved back to the United States. She landed in California for a bit, and we were lucky enough to have her at our church for a while, where I was able to get to know her. Lindsay has *no* problem with lordship. She has given Jesus full-blown access to her whole life. Lindsay moved back to America on her own because her heart broke for women affected by the sex trafficking industry. She had seen a video of a former prostitute who had prayed for God to save her from a drug overdose. When God saved this woman, she didn't know what to do next, but she figured going to the church for help was not an option because of her lifestyle. She didn't think she would be welcome. This woman's story broke

Lindsay's heart. You see, when Lindsay was 15 years old, God had showed her this verse in Luke 4:

> "The Spirit of the LORD is upon me, for he has anointed me to bring Good News to the poor. He has sent me to proclaim that captives will be released, that the blind will see, that the oppressed will be set free..."[7]

Something struck a chord with 15-year-old Lindsay and she felt like releasing captives and freeing the oppressed was what she was meant to give her life to doing. But at the time, it was just a bible verse. Lindsay didn't know what she was supposed to do with it. Years later, when she saw the video of the woman who was involved in prostitution, and she began developing a heart for those in the sex trafficking industry, Lindsay knew it was the fulfillment of the verse God had given her when she was 15.

Lindsay found her purpose, so it doesn't matter where God asks her to go, or what He asks her to do, she's in. Lindsay discovered who God has made her to be and how she can impact the world through her obedience to God.

But Lindsay didn't get her whole life plan dropped into her lap from the Lord. She got a bible verse, and then a decade later, she saw a video. Then Lindsay began to develop a heart to see people freed from trafficking. Following the internal prompting wasn't easy though. At 23 years old, she was working at her dream job in Ukraine, but knew she was being called to work against trafficking. Lindsay wondered, as many of us would have, why God would call her away from a near perfect situation to move away into one with more questions than answers. But then she felt God tell her, "there's nothing keeping you from doing it, so why don't you just go. If not now, then when?"

"Who am I to argue with God?" Lindsay asked herself. And so, she boarded a plane.

When she moved to California, she began to ask around about how she could help and started a ministry on the Central Coast. Lindsay has only been her for a year and has already decided to pack up and move again because God is calling her to a new ministry in Ridgecrest, California, 45 minutes away from a main hub for trafficking.

We were made to be set apart, to bring real solutions to real problems, to be a blessing to all people. Ask the women Lindsay is helping—and their families—how glad they are she's given Jesus lordship over her life. It's your risk-taking for the kingdom of God, empowered by the Holy Spirit, displayed in your community, that the world is waiting to see. Following Jesus can be risky, but it's also incredibly exciting to think how we've been adopted as sons and daughters into this new kingdom, and we get to partner with Him to see the reality of His kingdom revealed here on earth.

Chapter 5: Uber and the Kingdom

Years ago, when I was working for a medical company, I had to be in Las Vegas for a trade show. I'll be honest, I'm not a big fan—of trade shows *or* Vegas. But when I do stay in Las Vegas, I always stay downtown in Old Vegas. Maybe it's the low key vibe, away from the glitz and glamour of Las Vegas Boulevard, otherwise known as "The Strip." Maybe it's the local Arts District. Or maybe it's the $5-craps tables. Either way, downtown is my jam.

The only problem with staying downtown is the commute south to The Strip, where most conventions are hosted. Traffic can be bad, and it's just a hassle going back and forth. I would get an Uber to The Strip in the morning, back downtown after meetings, and again to The Strip for dinner with mucky-mucks, and then back downtown to hit the sack.

After four days in Las Vegas, it was time to head home. I'd had somewhere between 8-10 Uber drivers at that point. Most drivers were fairly talkative, which I think comes from a place of being hospitable and wanting to avoid awkward silence. Now, I don't know about you, but I don't mind silence. I've got two children, so my whole life is filled with noise. A 15 minute drive in silence sounds just dandy to me, but it makes most people uncomfortable, so I'm happy to carry on a conversation.

So, there I was. Standing outside my hotel, bags in hand, ready to go home and see my family again. I requested an Uber and five minutes later, Donald arrives. He was in his early twenties. He wore his Yankees hat low—just above his eyes—and spoke with a New York accent.

I threw my bags in the trunk and sat down in the passenger seat, preparing myself for the typical, "What are you here for?" types of questions, which came immediately. I answered Donald's questions and then, trying to even out the conversation, I asked him how his day was going.

His eyes lit up.

"Oh, man...this is the best day of my life. I mean, my kid being born was the best, but today is a great day."

"Oh, yeah," I replied. "Why?"

He spoke fast, like he couldn't get the story out quickly enough. "I'm from New York," he said. "I moved out here because I have a respiratory condition and the winters there were too hard on me. But my family is still there. I was born in New York, but my parents are from the Dominican Republic. They came into the United States illegally, so I've been trying to get my citizenship for two years. It's a long process," he explained.

Donald looked directly at me for a second and said, "I want to do it for my girlfriend and our kid, you know? So they can have a good life."

He explained to me how his girlfriend's mom didn't think much of him, and that she thinks her daughter could do better. Donald is respectful about the situation, but I could tell he had a chip on his shoulder about it and wanted to prove her wrong.

He continued the story: "After two years of going back and forth trying to get this sh—t taken care of, I got a call this morning that my citizenship was accepted. I literally just got off the phone 20 minutes ago with the guy. I'm so f—ing excited! Now I have to book a flight out to New York next week to take the oath and make it official." His phrase, "so f —ing excited" didn't even do it justice. I could see it all over his face. Pure joy.

And in that moment, driving to the airport in Las Vegas with my Uber driver, I was given the best representation of the gospel I had ever heard in my life.

Here was a guy who had come to a country he wasn't born into. He was a stranger here, looking for an identity— living within the walls, but needing to be adopted as a citizen...as a son. And now, after all those years, he had been accepted into the country he'd fought and sacrificed and traveled so long for.

Isn't that the way the kingdom of God works? You feel the spark...the pull. You hear the still, small voice of the King and begin walking towards the whisper a kingdom away.

The difference in the kingdom of God versus Donald's story is that when we hear the voice on the other end of the phone say, "you've been accepted," it wasn't *our* fighting and sacrifice that got us there. And when we look back on the miles we've traveled and the battles we've fought, we realize we crossed the border into the "new country" the moment we surrendered everything—the moment we gave Jesus lordship over our lives.

But the thing I'll always remember about Donald was that his being accepted brought him joy—and joy brought a declaration of allegiance. I was his first ride of the day, but I imagine everyone after me heard the same story. There's a joy that comes from being accepted and a security that comes from letting go. It's this upside-down thing about the kingdom where you surrender to the lordship of Jesus in your life and willingly become a slave to righteousness.

For my friend Lindsay, surrendering to the lordship of Jesus meant being willing to pack up and move out on a whim, because her life is not her own. You might not have a passion for trafficking, or need to move away, but what does surrendering to the lordship of Jesus look like for you? Maybe it's changing careers to do something that better utilizes your God-given passions and talents? Maybe it's simply praying for more opportunities to be a blessing where you are?

Perhaps you're a doctor and you're feeling the internal prompting to volunteer hours to a local homeless shelter. Perhaps you're like my wife and have been raising kids, but now they're in school for six hours a day. So, instead of vegging out, you make meals for people in need and invite other moms with younger kids to coffee so they can vent to someone who's been in their shoes, or clean someone's office at their work just because you know they'd appreciate it. (Seriously, my wife is a *boss*.) Maybe it's bringing a pint of ice cream to someone you know is struggling and just listening to them for a bit? Maybe it's bringing *me* a pint of ice cream...who knows!? God moves in mysterious ways! (If you do bring me ice cream, mint chip is my favorite, but that's neither here nor there.) The point is, how can you begin to take small steps in the direction of the internal prompting you're feeling? What is God speaking to you? Because He's *always* speaking! We just need ears to hear His voice.

PART II

THE VOICE

Chapter 6: Ruach

Ask any Christian you run into about the working and speaking of the Holy Spirit and you'll hear a wide range of beliefs. Some think the empowering of the Holy Spirit was limited to the first century church. On the other side of the spectrum, there's the thought that the Holy Spirit comes upon you, possesses your body, and you lose control. But for most of us, I'd say we land somewhere in the middle. We believe the Holy Spirit is alive and speaking, but at best, sounds only slightly more distinguishable than the "wah-wah" voice of adults in *Peanuts* cartoons.

But if we are going to rediscover the purpose for which we were created, we must be submitted to the lordship of Jesus, empowered by the Holy Spirit, and engaged in our community. We've talked about the lordship of Jesus, so now let's focus on being empowered by the Holy Spirit.

Before we get into the function of the Holy Spirit, we have to understand who the Holy Spirit is. Depending on our backgrounds, we might come into this conversation with very different opinions and beliefs about the Holy Spirit, which is normal. Many of our beliefs are shaped by our upbringing and culture. But when we're talking about God and His impact in our lives and communities, it's critical that our beliefs are shaped by scripture—both for ourselves and for those we speak to—so we can paint a clear picture of the God we want the introduce them to. To be frank, there's just some straight up bad theology concerning the Holy Spirit out there, and my fear is that we Christians are responsible for much of the confusion. So, it's also our job to clear it up and help each other—and those who don't yet know God—to understand Him as best we can.

If someone is talking trash about a person you love, and the reality is that their beliefs about the person are rooted in half-truths and assumptions, wouldn't you want to set them straight? Wouldn't you want to say, "Hold on a

second....you don't know this person like I know them! Let

me tell you about them..."? It's the same thing with God. We

must root our beliefs and conversations in the scriptures

so we, and others, are seeing God the Father, the Son, and

the Spirit through the right lens. So, let's dig into the biblical

understanding of the Holy Spirit so we have the correct

context for the rest of the conversation.

Can you guess where in the Bible the Holy Spirit is first

introduced? The second verse! That's right, Genesis 1:1

introduces us to God, who created the heavens and the

earth, and then in verse 2, we read:

> The earth was without form, and void; and
>
> darkness was on the face of the deep. And
>
> the Spirit of God was hovering over the face
>
> of the waters.

This verse teaches us so much about the person and function of the Spirit—and is reinforced throughout the rest of the Old and New Testaments. We're just going to look at a few of the many verses that show a consistent function of the Spirit.

Noticing how people function in their context helps paint a picture of who they are and what they care about. We do it with each other all the time. We look at the habits, actions, and passions of a person—what they do for work and what they do with their free time—and it helps us understand a bit of who they are. Look at the profile pictures of people on social media and you'll get an idea of what's important to them. Are they wearing a jersey of their favorite sports team, hiking in a national park, or posing for a corporate headshot? Or maybe it's that shirtless dude on Tinder, or the guy riding a unicorn? Whatever it is, we're looking for an understanding of the person through the context of what they do. It's the same when we meet someone in person for the first time. What's one of the first questions we ask?

"*What do you do?*" Knowing what people do may help us understand who they are. We can also carry this practice into the scriptures by looking at the actions of Jesus and the Spirit of God.

To begin clarifying who the Holy Spirit is, let's begin by looking at the name. In Genesis 1:2, the word "Spirit" in Hebrew, (which is the original language of the Old Testament) is *ruach*, which means "wind," or "breath."

Genesis 1:2 could be translated as:

> The earth was without form, and void; and darkness was on the face of the deep. And the *breath/wind of God* was hovering over the face of the waters.

I think this is so cool. Check this out. The next time we see the word *ruach* is in Genesis 3:8:

> 8And they heard the voice of the Lord God walking in the garden in the cool of the day: and Adam and his wife hid themselves from the presence of the Lord God amongst the trees of the garden.

The phrase "in the cool" is that word, *ruach*. Let's read it again.

> 8And they heard the voice of the Lord God walking in the garden in the breath/wind (*ruach*) of the day: and Adam and his wife hid themselves from the presence of the Lord God amongst the trees of the garden.

Adam and Eve heard the voice of the Lord in the breath of the day. It's beautiful imagery.

Before this verse, Adam and Eve had just done the one thing God commanded them not to do. God gave them everything they could have wanted. He just told them not to eat from this one tree—the tree of the knowledge of good and evil. God wanted humanity to understand good and evil on His terms, how He sees it. But humanity decided to seize control and define good and evil ourselves. Sin entered God's good world and we've been trying to define good and evil ourselves ever since.

Adam and Eve were ashamed at their decision and hid from God. They heard the "voice" of God as He walked in the "breath/wind" of the day. This might have been a regular scene, but this instance would be the last time God walked with man until Jesus comes on the scene. It's a beautiful picture because it seems as if this is the way it was always intended to be—that we hear the voice of God in the breath of the day, that the very wind was meant to carry the voice of God throughout His good world.

That's how the Bible identifies the Spirit of God, as God's breath. Now that we understand the name of the Spirit, we're going to get into the function of the Spirit. So, back to Genesis 1:2, where we are introduced to the Spirit of God, who is "hovering" over the waters. The word "hovers" is the Hebrew word *rachaph*, which is a verb that can be translated into English as: "to move, flutter, hover, or shake." It can also be translated "to brood." You see, in order to properly understand the Holy Spirit, you have to understand chickens.

I know that's a hard left turn, but follow me on this one. My wife and I have had chickens for years. Our relationship with our chickens was purely utilitarian. We fed them and they gave us eggs. But it turns out, hens are incredible parents. They will go to great lengths to make sure their eggs hatch and grow into adult chickens, able to fend for themselves. Mother hens become very suspicious of new hens that enter the group, even to the point of pecking the new hens to death! Mother hens will also peck holes in the shells of the eggs of other hens so that their eggs never develop and their young have more food and resources for themselves. Really intense stuff! But the point here is they are ultra-committed to their young. So, what does this have to do with the Spirit of God? Well, I mentioned the word *rachaph* can be translated as "to brood." We could read Genesis 1:2 to say that the Spirit of God "brooded over the face of the waters."

Often, when a mother hen has laid an egg and won't get off it, she is said to be "broody." I've experienced this myself. Some varieties of hens are more likely to become broody than others, but you know it when you see it. Like I said, our relationship with these hens was utilitarian. We wanted eggs for breakfast, so we didn't have any roosters to fertilize the eggs and make baby chickens, but the hens didn't know that. They were going to hover over those eggs regardless. If you try to take an egg from a broody hen, you will regret it. They make an awful screeching noise, shake and ruffle their feathers to appear larger and more intimidating, and if you reach your hand into the nesting box of a broody hen, you will get pecked almost immediately. In fact, in order to get the eggs from a broody hen, I would have to grab a stick and physically push her off the egg, which required more strength than you'd expect. These hens were committed to the birthing of their offspring.

This imagery really helps me when thinking about the Spirit of God, brooding over the face of the waters, committed to the birthing of this new world that God the Father was about to speak into existence. It's almost as if the Spirit acts as an incubator over creation, ready to energize and give power to the thing that God the Father speaks over. Interestingly, you even see Jesus use the language of a broody hen in Matthew chapter 23, verse 37. Jesus is angry with the Pharisees and religious leaders of the day, explaining to them that they've killed the prophets and others he's sent to them throughout Israel's journey. The whole time, Jesus longed to gather their children together, "as a hen gathers her chicks under her wings," but they were not willing.

The Holy Spirit gives life, energizing and empowering that which the Father speaks. Throughout scripture, we often read about God's voice and the Spirit, which we understand to be the "breath of God." So, we've got the voice and the breath. What's the difference? Think about this for a moment. When you speak, your "voice" interrupts the air molecules in front of your mouth, creating waves which are then perceived as sound by the auditory and central nervous system of the person within range of the waves. That's how we would "hear" a voice or any other sound.

But there's another element at play here. Put your hand in front of your mouth as you speak. You'll "hear" your voice, but there's something else that's not related to audible sound. It's more tactile—something you feel or experience.

It's the movement of your voice—it's your "breath." This is a good way of thinking about the relationship between the voice of God and the breath (Spirit) of God. If you're like me, you're asking yourself, "so...are your voice and your breath the same, or are they different?" Exactly! They're the same *and* distinctly different. When you speak you experience the breath, but they're also uniquely different in effect. It's the same with the relationship between God and His Spirit.

The energizing and empowering work of the Holy Spirit is critical when it comes to establishing the kingdom of God here on earth. For whatever reason, God chose to do that work through *us*—those who have made Jesus Lord of our lives and have become slaves to the work of restoring and redeeming His good world. As we begin to rediscover how God has set us apart—made us different, uniquely ourselves—we'll begin to walk in the direction of that prompting. As we being walking, the Holy Spirit will empower our actions so that everything we do can have a transformational effect on those we impact. Remember that every vocation, every action, can be sacred when it's co-opted by the kingdom through the empowering of the Holy Spirit. We are never *just* anything when we're doing it for the kingdom. But how do we actually hear the voice of God through the Holy Spirit? How does it all work? And why is obedience to that voice critical?

I've got two young kids. Often, when I ask my son to clean his room or make his bed, he'll respond with, "I knooooooow, Dad." To which I reply, "Well, if you knew, you would have done it." He can tell me he knows what he's *supposed* to do all day long, but the evidence of *understanding* is action.

Jesus spoke about this in Luke 6:46: "So why do you keep calling me 'Lord, Lord!' when you don't do what I say?"

Again, the evidence of understanding is action. *Obedience.*

But the truth is, many of us don't recognize the voice of the Holy Spirit. Lord knows I didn't for the longest time. Sure, I was a Christian and He was speaking, but it's like trying to pick a voice you've never heard out of a crowd. However, if we are going to rediscover our purpose in this world and walk in the power of the Spirit, we *must* learn to recognize the voice of the Spirit. So much of what I believe God wants to do through us is to meet the needs of others. When I look at Jesus' life, He was constantly meeting needs. Sometimes those needs were physical (feeding the multitudes), sometimes they were spiritual (casting out demons), and often, they were miraculous (healing the sick and raising the dead). In the fourteenth chapter of John, Jesus says:

> "Most assuredly, I say to you, he who believes in Me, the works that I do he will do also; and greater works than these he will do, because I go to My Father."[1]

Because Jesus was glorified, defeated death, went to the Father, and sent the Holy Spirit, we can now partner with Him to do the works He did to establish His kingdom here on earth. If we are listening to the Holy Spirit, I believe He will make the need clear, and then provide the power to fulfill it.

Even Jesus only did what the Father told Him to do. It was about listening and being obedient.

But how do we begin to hear the voice of the Spirit?

Chapter 7: How We Listen

I can pick my wife's voice out of a crowd because I've spent years and years listening to it. Her voice is now distinguishable amongst other voices. Even more nuanced than her voice are the looks she gives me—which aren't always subtle! If you've been in a relationship long enough, maybe you've had the experience of your partner giving you "the look," that means it's time to go. You can almost feel them looking at you before you make eye contact. I believe the Spirit wants to have this kind of relationship with us as well.

After church on Sundays, our congregation meets outside to get a cup of coffee and catch up with each other. There's typically over a hundred people outside and the kids are running around screaming like banshees. It's controlled chaos. But when one of my kids is looking for me and yells, "Dad!" It doesn't matter what I'm doing or who I'm talking to, my ears perk up and my head turns to get my eyes on them. Most every man out there is a dad, and their kids use the same three letters to call them as well. But I know when *my* kid calls me.

In John 10:27, Jesus says, "My sheep hear my voice..." I believe the same concept applies for the Holy Spirit, since the Spirit is the breath of the Father. But again, how do we recognize a voice we aren't familiar with? I wish I had an exciting answer, but I don't. The truth is, I believe it simply comes from time spent listening for the voice. And please don't think I'm an expert on this by any means. I'm still learning. But I've become convinced that fulfilling the mission of Jesus here on earth, and in doing so, seeing the "pink flamingo" come back to life, is done through the hard work of listening and obeying.

Sometimes God speaks audibly to us on His own, sometimes through our friends, or even through a donkey (if you're *really* stubborn).[1] But for many of us, hearing the voice of the Lord is something that takes time—and that relationship is built alone in quiet places. I would encourage all of you to wake up early or stay up late—but spend quiet time alone with the Lord, reading the scriptures and just...listening. For me, this means waking up before the kids are awake, pouring a cup of coffee and opening the Bible.

While I love the feel of an actual, paper Bible, there's something so dynamic and productive about all of the Bible apps available on our devices. I'll switch back and forth, but for the most part, I'll choose a reading plan available through many of the apps and pick up where I left off the day before. These apps can give you reminders, and even read the Bible to you, if you prefer. Whatever you choose, the goal is time alone with the scriptures, asking the Holy Spirit to speak to you through them. With as much stimulation as we've got coming at us constantly, listening can be difficult. I tend to find reasons to create distraction when I'm trying to listen. But silence is a gift! And it's one we can create in order to listen to the still, small voice of the Spirit. It doesn't take much. Most days, I'll only spend 30 minutes alone. Just spend the time you have. God will use it, because it doesn't matter how *long* we listen, it's about *how* we listen. We need to listen differently. We've been conditioned to read and listen for content—for knowledge—which is great, but incomplete. We've also got to listen and read for revelation—how Jesus wants to encounter us in our own lives through the stories in scripture. That's the stuff that really changes things. The Pharisees knew a lot about scripture. Even demons recognize the voice of Jesus. But those who had an encounter with Jesus were *transformed*. And isn't that what we all want anyway?

In time, as He speaks, you will begin to recognize His voice. But hearing is only the first step—the trick is in the obedience. Remember though, the point of obedience is for God to meet the needs of others through our obedience—to see His kingdom revealed here on earth—and that is exciting. The testimonies I've collected in my own life when I've been obedient to the voice of the Lord just blow my mind. They prove His faithfulness and proclaim His goodness!

When we are all operating in that kind of power, through the prompting of the Spirit, I guarantee you, we will not wonder what sets us apart any longer. I can't say we will always be liked, but our interactions with others will go from transactional to transformational, and we will realize this is what we were created for—to reveal the reality of the kingdom of God in and through our lives.

However, this journey towards hearing can be tedious, and it requires discipline. A few years ago, I wasn't reading my Bible much at all. I had this great excuse though. I told myself, "I don't want to read the Bible until I *want* to read the Bible." I was telling myself that I was disrespecting the

Lord by reading the Bible out of discipline rather than passion. Really, I was just being lazy. Husbands, it's like when your wife says, "I just want you to *want* to do the dishes." The truth is, it just ain't gonna happen! Who likes doing the dishes? We've got to do them out of discipline and respect.

My wife and I have gone through marriage counseling several times. Sometimes when we were in a healthy place and sometimes when we were not. Let's face it, marriage is tough and it's important to seek guidance and counsel from people with more wisdom and experience than you. (Can I get a witness?) When we first started going to counseling, I was really clueless and thought, *Finally someone is going to tell my wife how lucky she is to have a husband like me!* Well, let's just say that it didn't happen quite like that. Talk about being humbled.

But in one of our meetings, the counselors asked us if we ever held hands. My wife and I weren't very "touchy-feely," so we didn't hold hands much. We just didn't "feel" like it—the passion wasn't there. Our counselors encouraged us to try it, to hold hands as we were walking down the street, and see if the passion would come in time.

I think it's often the same way with our spiritual lives. So, I decided to implement that principle into my own spiritual journey. I began to read the Bible consistently, out of discipline. I would wake up and pour over the scriptures—reading for revelation and encounter. I prayed the Spirit would speak to me. I researched the original language. I thought about the context the authors were living in. I read *differently*. And guess what? Passion began to come out of the discipline! Now, my passion drives my discipline to stay in the Word.

I can't tell you how much I get out of my time with the Lord, in the scriptures and prayer. And the Spirit has been faithful to teach and guide and reveal truth to me in those times and throughout the day—when I actually stop and

make room for Him!

PART III

THE CITY

Chapter 8: Shepherd King

"And in the end, it'll just be you and Jesus."

Said no scripture *ever*.

I'm sure you've heard it before. Those Christians who don't think they need people around them. "It's just me and Jesus," they say. Most of us have been there before. Whether it's from getting burned by other people, ministry, or just burned out on life, we have a tendency to disengage with the people around us. Because let's be honest...it's easier that way! But our calling is to help form disciples who usher in a new kingdom. And it takes disciples to form disciples.

Truth be told, I need people around me as well. People that will hold me accountable, encourage me, and show up, even when I don't want them to. We all need people like that. In the end, our King won't usher in an island, He will usher in a new city, which the Bible calls, "The New Jerusalem."[1]

God's goal is, and has always been, to have Heaven and Earth overlap. In Matthew 6, Jesus prayed, "*Thy kingdom come, Thy will be done in earth, as it is in heaven.*"[2] In the end, Jesus will consecrate them as one. This passage from Revelation 21 describes that moment:

> [1]Now I saw a new heaven and a new earth, for the first heaven and the first earth had passed away. Also there was no more sea. [2]Then I, John, saw the holy city, New Jerusalem, coming down out of heaven from God, prepared as a bride adorned for her husband. [3]And I heard a loud voice from heaven saying, "Behold, the tabernacle of God is with men, and He will dwell with them,

and they shall be His people. God Himself will
be with them and be their God."

God is building a city. This is really important. In the Gospel
of Matthew, Jesus says,

> [14]You are the light of the world. A city set on a
> hill cannot be hidden; [15]nor does anyone light
> a lamp and put it under a basket, but on the
> lampstand, and it gives light to all who are in
> the house. [16]Let your light shine before men in
> such a way that they may see your good
> works, and glorify your Father who is in
> heaven.[3]

What Adam and Eve began in a garden, we will see made
whole in a city. Read the passage again. See that phrase
"city on a hill?"

We tend to read "city," but think "church." But it doesn't say a "church on a hill," it says a "city on a hill." I believe the mark of a healthy church is a healthy city. Cities with healthy churches should have lower crime rates, better education, sustainable business practices, and programs for helping the weak and marginalized. The beauty and miracle of the local church is that there are a bunch of people who are different in age, race, profession, and political beliefs coming together, saying, "we are going to be set apart for the cause of Christ. We are going to operate differently in order to be a blessing to our community."

When the world looks in on the church with all of our quirks and diversity and wonders how it's possible, we can point to Jesus and say, "it's because of what Jesus did for us. We love because He first loved us." Our communities should be better off for having a healthy church within its borders. It goes back to the question my pastor asks us: "If we were to close our doors tomorrow, who besides the people who come to our church would even care?" We need to help our cities and communities shine so brightly that they cannot be hidden. The goal isn't simply that our city would shine, but that other cities would see the light and do the same—so that the kingdom of heaven would spread throughout God's good world.

The intention of the gospel is that it spreads beyond the walls of our church buildings. Healthy churches should, both by instinct and intention, be working diligently to culture healthy communities that more and more closely resemble the kingdom of God. Instinctively, meaning we work towards healthy individuals and communities because it's part of our new nature as Christians. We just instinctively identify and influence situations for the improvement of our communities. But there also needs to be an intention—a determination—to identify the weak and marginalized, the hurting and broken, and work diligently to foster health and wholeness. These needs will likely vary slightly from community to community, but I would hope the church makes it their mission to see health and wholeness restored to broken situations within the context of their own communities.

We're seeing it already. The generation coming up has a huge appetite for social justice and seeing change in their communities—both of which are very healthy. And their goal isn't to slap a spiritual Band-Aid on people or entire communities. They realize it's time to roll up their sleeves and do the hard work of creating solutions that provide real, lasting, deep healing. Healing that shelters the homeless, feeds the hungry, empowers women, builds bridges across political ideologies, and seeks to repair race relationships. Most American churches aren't talking about the things most Americans are actually dealing with, and I believe our silence is to our own detriment. Poverty, sexuality, social justice, education, racism, and many others are serious issues requiring serious dialogue. And if the church doesn't engage culture in ways that embody the compassion, wisdom, and truth of Jesus, the church will never become a source of healing.

The need for the church to go beyond simply being a place of meeting is more important than ever. Jesus Christ is the hope of the world, and for better or worse, He handed the mission and message to us. But He also gave us a secret weapon called the Holy Spirit to empower us to do the work of ushering in His kingdom.

We live in a post-Christian culture. More and more people in our communities haven't grown up with the beliefs and traditions that those of us who grew up in the Christian church are so deeply ingrained in. Many don't even have a peripheral understanding of the biblical narrative that would give them context for the message of Jesus. This makes inviting nonbelievers to come to church to "get saved" a difficult proposition, especially as a first step. I'm not saying it never happens. What I'm saying is that if we have any chance of making disciples, of being a blessing to our communities, we've got to do it on neutral turf—in homes and businesses—in the context of real relationship.

Let me tell you a story about ice cream.

Greg Steinberger grew up in Wisconsin. It's cold in Wisconsin, so after high school, Greg joined the Navy because he thought they would go to warm places. After eight years in the Navy, Greg ended up in the Bay Area of California with a master's degree in Business Administration. He worked in the corporate world for years, mostly in Human Resources, and he hated it. Greg had taken a talent assessment years before and had since forgotten all about it. When he pulled out the assessment again, he realized that out of 11 possible career fields suited to his strengths, Human Resources was ranked 10th. He was in the wrong field, and he knew it. Not only that, Greg had just gone through his second divorce and was on the verge of a complete breakdown.

So, when Greg was invited by a friend to a Christian men's retreat, he thought, *Why not? I've got nothing left to lose.* Greg was raised Catholic but only went to church on Easter and Christmas, so he didn't have a framework for any real kind of faith. When he got to the retreat, he realized these guys were hardcore Christians. He felt like he was in the wrong place, especially when it came time for the prayer meeting. It was one of those prayer meetings where someone begins the prayer time and then towards the end, asks people to speak out and share what they're struggling with so they can be prayed for. After a long, awkward pause with no one being willing to share, the leader interrupted the silence saying, "I think there's one more story here that needs to be shared." I've been a Christian my whole life, and those kinds of prayer meetings still terrify me! But someone in the room shared a story about letting go, and Greg knew it was for him. You see,

Greg's second divorce was a result of his not being able to let go of his first wife, who had died in a plane crash. His second wife left him, saying, "I can't compete with a ghost."

While he was in the prayer meeting, Greg remembered hearing a story of how African hunters caught wild monkeys. They'd stick a banana in a jar and anchor the jar to a log. When a monkey would come by, it would stick its hand in the jar, grab the banana and get stuck because the monkey wouldn't let go of the banana to get its hand back out, even if it meant captivity. Greg knew he had to let go, but he didn't know how. He walked out of the prayer meeting onto the outside lawn and literally felt Jesus' presence lifting him up. "I felt like I could just jump up and fly," Greg said. He was out there on the lawn for 20 minutes, at times feeling pure relief, and at times dropping to his knees unable to stand. Greg was 37 years old and had just surrendered to the lordship of Christ.

Not knowing what to do with his new-found freedom, Greg decided to travel across the country visiting friends and family and living out of his car. After five months of bumming around the country, Greg remembered he had an all-expense paid trip to Costa Rica from his previous job he had postponed. He boarded a plane in search of purpose and adventure.

After ten days in Costa Rica, on the night he was supposed to fly back, Greg wondered what he was going back to. There was nothing for him in the States, so he pushed his flight back, all the while praying about how he might use the talents God had given him.

One day while still in Costa Rica, Greg had a craving for ice cream. The only issue was, he couldn't find any! *That's it,* Greg thought. *I'll be the Ben & Jerry's of Costa Rica!* But there were two problems with that plan—Greg didn't know how to speak Spanish, and Greg didn't know how to make ice cream. He got back on a plane to America to learn how to speak Spanish and make ice cream.

Months passed, and Greg had taken his second and third trip to Costa Rica, trying to launch his ice cream shop, but nothing was working out. He wasn't catching onto the language, the lease on the business property he had his eye on fell through, and Greg decided to give up.

He had always wanted to live on the Central Coast in California. He had been there several times throughout his life and thought it would be the perfect place to live. After moving to the Central Coast, he found himself walking downtown in the small village of Arroyo Grande— distraught with his failure—when he looked up and saw an ice cream parlor called Burnardoz. Greg thought, *What the heck?* and walked through the door to ask the owner of the ice cream shop, who had been in that location for 27 years, if he would be willing to sell the business to him.

The owner replied, "Funny you should ask, I'm meeting with my lawyer in two hours to talk about my options." It turned out he was getting evicted.

Greg couldn't believe it!

You see, the "failed" business venture in Costa Rica had done two things. God used it to see if Greg would be obedient to follow His lead. But it also provided some time to pass so things back in America could fall into place. Six months prior, the owner of Burnardoz wasn't looking to sell at all.

Greg went to work. He asked Mr. Burns, the original founder of Burnardoz who had a thriving business in the past, to come out of retirement to teach him how to make ice cream and run a successful company. He changed the name of the company from Burnardoz to Doc Burnstein's, a combination of their two last names. But after two years, Doc Burnstein's was still losing money.

One day, a mom came into the ice cream shop asking if she could put a money collection box at the counter for her infant son who had health issues. Greg didn't want to, but feeling compassion for the woman and her son, he agreed. But then Greg thought, *We should do something more than just a collection box. Maybe a percentage of sales?* Greg heard an internal prompt saying, *Do more.* But Greg thought,

I can't do more...I can't afford more, we're already losing money.

Greg heard again, *Do more.*

"What if we gave 50% of sales?" Greg said.

Greg heard again, *Do more.*

Greg decided to take a big risk and walked in the direction of the internal prompt. He announced Baby Austyn Day, a day in which 100% of sales went to this baby boy and his mom. Baby Austyn Day turned out to be their biggest sales day ever—and yet they didn't make a dime. But that day was pivotal for Greg and the future of Doc Burnstein's Ice Cream Lab because it transformed what Greg thought the business was for. He realized its purpose wasn't simply to sell ice cream.

It was to be a beacon of hope in the community—to help create a city on a hill.

Baby Austyn died at 18 months of age, but what Austyn and Greg were able to do together continues to this day. Over fourteen years later, Doc Burnstein's Ice Cream Lab is still helping to create a city on a hill. Greg gives 10% of all profits back to the community and every August, they have a day of giving back where, just like Baby Austyn Day, 100% of sales goes into a scholarship to help people in the community.

Any vocation—even ice cream—can be sacred if it's co-opted by the kingdom. You are never *just* anything when you're doing it for the kingdom. Doc Burnstein's has been a driving force for community improvement all because Greg was obedient. But the thing is, Greg didn't have a master plan of community transformation when he started. He got two words at a time: "Costa Rica," "ice cream," "Central Coast," "Do more," and so on. Greg listened to and obeyed the voice of the Holy Spirit, and God took over and did what only God can do. Greg says, "don't pray for *how* to get there, just set your attention on the Lord." Greg didn't have an overwhelming sense of confidence along the way. In fact, he just told me the other day, "I still don't know what I'm doing." But God has done immeasurably more through this little ice cream shop than Greg could have asked or imagined. I wonder how your little acts of obedience might transform your own community if you'd only take the risk of radical obedience?

Chapter 9: Six Doors

Now, maybe you're not passionate about ice cream, or trafficking, or leading a church. But I would suspect there's something that you love and are called to do, even if you can't quite pinpoint it yet. For me, it was always playing music. Or, at least I thought it was. I would have sworn to you that playing music was the thing God wanted me to do with my life. And somewhere along the way, I developed some bad theology. I thought whatever I loved the most, that was the thing I had to sacrifice. Because of my deep love for music, this thought terrified me.

Now there are biblical examples of doing exactly that throughout scripture; Abraham being asked to sacrifice Isaac is perhaps the most famous. But we have this terrible problem in the church of taking singular examples in scripture and applying them as general biblical principles. Or the opposite problem, where things meant to be biblical principles are dismissed as isolated events (i.e.,

God performed miracles through the disciples, but not through modern day people like us).

In any case, I had this theology that convinced me I had to sacrifice the thing I loved most which, in my case, was playing music. I was in a band in high school, started leading worship in college, recorded a few albums, and the thought of giving it up was disheartening, to say the least. But in some misguided effort to please God, I was willing to. Tell me this though, how many of you would tell your children they need to give up all their toys to prove they love you? That would be *super* messed up!

One day in college, like a bolt of lightning from heaven, a thought occurred to me that changed everything. I thought, *Wait....who put this passion in me in the first place?*

I believe the Lord gives each of us talents and abilities to use to glorify Him through our lives. When you accept that, it will change the way you think about your life. Every one of us is unique and, like the plastic pink flamingo, was meant to be a real solution to some of the world's real problems. God has created you to be and carry an expression of Himself that no one else can, or will ever carry again on earth. Maybe you don't know what it is yet, but there's something uniquely you that God wants to see released in your community.

I've been talking a lot about listening to the Holy Spirit. Sometimes it just takes a while to separate the signal from the noise. As I've been learning to hear His voice, I've realized He's been speaking the whole time. He's been confirming everything I've known to be true about myself. That I've not been fearfully and wonderfully made to be average. You either. So, what *are* you made for? Only you can answer that. But it's probably that thing you feel deep down in your bones—the thing you can't *not* do. And if you won't do it for yourself—do it for me. Your risk-taking for the kingdom of God, empowered by the Holy Spirit, displayed in your communities, is what the world is waiting to see!

I used to think that life was about finding the *one* thing you were passionate about. Once you found your passion, you were to embrace it and run. For me, at the time, it was music. For years, my life was consumed with figuring out how to play music full-time, finding a way to become successful through this thing I loved so much. I didn't realize it then, but my happiness hinged on the progress of my music career, which was basically nonexistent. Turns out, I'm not all that good! But I was trying *so* hard to make something happen, to create a career out of thin air. My biggest fear was that I would miss the one opportunity that would launch me into the stratosphere. This way of thinking was killing me. Any musician will tell you that the music business is like a rollercoaster. Some days you're up, and some days you're down. Imagine if your emotions followed this pattern. Maybe some of yours do! In any case, it makes for a very stressful, very unfulfilled life. You are constantly redefining success and failure in a never ending attempt to reach the carrot dangling in front of you.

One night, completely distraught over my failed attempts to become a full-time musician, I remember asking God something like, "Just show me the door, and I'll walk through it." Immediately after the words left my mouth, a deep realization hit...followed by the weightiness telling me there was some truth to it. It was like God was telling me, "Maybe there's not just one door. Maybe there are six." God was telling me that He would bless *any* of the six doors. He just wanted me to walk, to *do something*. To walk in the way of the internal promptings. I had become paralyzed by fear and couldn't move forward unless I was stepping into fame and fortune. But God was telling me that the door I chose wasn't as important as just taking the first step. I had forgotten I'd chosen to follow a God who is bigger than my mistakes. I'm continually amazed at God's ability to weave together something beautiful out of my fumbling attempts to follow Him.

So, how did it work out for me, you ask? Well, I never did become a professional musician. I spent the next twelve years in business. I learned how to lead. I learned how to be strategic and plan (things most musicians struggle with). I learned how to communicate and tell a story. And I got pretty good at business. I had the big title and the big money, but I was a fish out of water. I never felt comfortable in the boardroom. Toward the end of my career in business, I knew I was in a transition. I knew my time with the company I had been with for so long was coming to an end. Not only that, I knew God was calling me out of business altogether. He was calling me to the church. This wasn't necessarily good news for me. I had opportunities to switch careers and go into paid ministry a few times before and had successfully avoided it. I didn't want anything to do with working for a church. I had seen enough of it, and what I saw made my stomach turn. In business, there are rules. Budgets get set, decisions get made, and you execute—whether you like it or not. But in the church, everyone has an opinion of how the church should be run—and often we fight to the death over things that have very little to do with the gospel. Church ministry can be ugly. You often see the worst of people, the dark underbelly of the church. But the church was exactly what God was calling me into.

Over my last year in business, I just knew that I knew that I knew, God was calling me to the church. Not to come with the answers—but to start conversations. Over the years, I had been mentored by some amazing men—I had done a lot of growing up. My relationship with the Lord had gotten stronger, and I had never been more certain about who I was and what I was made to do. After years of training and growing, it was finally time to run.

And then I got laid off.

Chapter 10: Pivot

When our Chief Operating Officer (whom I reported to) called me into her office for our weekly one-on-one and indicated she had the Vice President of Human Resources with her in the room, I knew what was about to happen. The company hadn't been doing well for years, and she really wanted my position (which I was fulfilling remotely) to be relocated to our corporate office in San Francisco. I was laid off with three months' severance. I felt a strange mixture of emotions. Oddly, fear wasn't one of them. I knew God was in this change. I had submitted to the lordship of Jesus and had been given a gift of faith for the next season.

I resisted the urge to panic. I had been working part-time at our church as Interim Director for the Worship Department, so I did have some money coming in to help keep us afloat. I also knew I was supposed to write this book. I committed myself to diligently write, not seek out the next job in business that would inevitably take me away from my family and passions again. That season of my life was over.

Don't get me wrong, there were still more questions than answers, but I had faith. I committed myself to trust God for the future, even though on paper, it didn't look good. God's favor looked a lot like failure, but I didn't see it that way. Remember the story in Mark 4 where Jesus calms the storm? Well, Jesus was napping during that storm. If Jesus is supposed to be our teacher, showing us how to live, then we should try to model his behavior, right? Jesus took a posture of rest in the midst of the storm. He was able to do this because He knew His Father was good, and He knew His authority as a son. Jesus woke up, calmed the storm, and rebuked His disciples for their lack of faith.

Here's the thing though: many of these guys were fisherman. They fished on boats...that had sails. I know what you're probably thinking: "Thank you, Captain Obvious," right? But think about it. These men were acutely aware of how the wind and the waves affected their success or failure. For them, this wasn't a biblical concept like it has become for us. They had seen firsthand the destruction storms can bring. The wind and waves literally dictated whether they'd have a catch that day or not, and if there was no catch, there was no money. The sea was their professional environment. So, yes, Jesus commands natural things, but we also have to believe that, like the wind and the waves for the fisherman, He also commands the environments we live and work in as well.

The way my business career came to an end is a testimony to God's faithfulness. I probably would have *never* left the company I was with. I had become so comfortable. I knew the job well, and the salary was enough to give my family a comfortable life. Even though I knew it was time to move on, and I had a pretty good idea of what the next step would be, I was stuck…frozen in my comfort. I wonder if any of you are in the same place right now?

About a month after being laid off, I was at my son's baseball practice, and my phone started blowing up. Messages were coming in from the coworkers still with the company I had been with. They were texting me to let me know the company had just been sold to a private equity firm out of New York. The firm had gutted the place, taking it from 1,000 down to 300 employees nearly overnight. What's worse, if an employee had been with the company for over a year, they would only receive two weeks of severance pay. Two weeks! I felt terrible for my friends, but also thankful I had received what ended up being the best deal anyone had received. God had, once again, shown me that what looked like failure was actually His favor. Remember though, I didn't choose to leave. I was laid off. It's not like I get some "Big Faith" award or anything. And I'm certainly not saying anyone should quit their jobs. I'm just saying, you need to be braver than I was, in whatever capacity that means for your life.

I don't know exactly what's next, but God has proven Himself faithful over and over again. I can't look back on the things He's done, and say, "but I don't trust You for the next thing." This season has been harder than we ever thought possible, but has brought me more confidence in the Lord than I have ever known.

For me, living a God-sized life means communicating to and with the church. To connect people to ideas. To start conversations. To help make disciples. Even when I thought it was music, it turned out that leading worship was only another avenue for me to communicate with the church. But my "thing" the whole time was communicating. For you, it's probably different. But for both our sakes, find out what it is and run after it.

There's a reason the Bible describes the collective group of Christ-followers as "the body." The kingdom of God advances most efficiently and effectively when every Christ-follower is operating in the capacity they are designed for, and in partnership with other Christ-followers —like the human body. And not everyone needs to be a finger or a foot, or have an outward facing function. I'm learning that some of the biggest kingdom advancers are the behind-the-scenes builders and encouragers. Those that simply take the time to speak the life-giving truth of the gospel to those that need to hear it. They are the intercessors, the prayer warriors, the Spirit whisperers— those that act as the heart or lungs, pumping life into the rest of the body. God bless all of you! Keep doing your behind-the-scenes, introverted, organization-designing, nature-walking, food-making, system-building, baby-holding, prayer-closet kingdom thing! The point is, whatever God calls you to, it isn't just for you. It's for those in the boat.

Chapter 11: Those in the Boat

I heard an interview with Scott Harrison, CEO and founder of a non-profit called charity: water. Their mission is to bring clean, safe drinking water to people in developing countries. Their business model is really interesting in that private donors cover their operating costs, so 100% of donations will go straight to bringing clean water to people in need. Listening to Scott talk about charity: water was so interesting because it wasn't even about charity: water. I mean, it was in that they are the conduit for clean water, but it was always about others—about the people in need. Scott's heart broke for the people affected by dirty drinking water and he set out to do something about it. When we discover our purpose, it is never for ourselves, although we get to enjoy being used by God. Our purpose is always to be a blessing to others. Check out this example from Matthew 14:

> 22Immediately Jesus made the disciples get into the boat and go on ahead of him to the other side, while he dismissed the crowd.

23After he had dismissed them, he went up on a mountainside by himself to pray. Later that night, he was there alone, 24and the boat was already a considerable distance from land, buffeted by the waves because the wind was against it.[1]

Okay, so let's pause here to really understand the scene. Jesus has just fed 5,000 people with five loaves of bread and two fish. After dinner, Jesus sends the disciples away in a boat to the other side of the lake because he wants to be alone and pray. I wonder if they thought, *Wait...Jesus, how are you going to get to the other side of the lake if we've got the boat?* Maybe they thought he'd just walk the long way around? But Jesus had other plans.

Night falls and the disciples are in big trouble. They battle strong winds and heavy waves *all* night, likely wondering why Jesus just performed a miracle on the land only to let them die on the water. Then...

> 25Shortly before dawn Jesus went out to them, walking on the lake. 26When the disciples saw him walking on the lake, they were terrified. "It's a ghost," they said, and cried out in fear. 27But Jesus immediately said to them: "Take courage! It is I. Don't be afraid." 28"Lord, if it's you," Peter replied, "tell me to come to you on the water." 29"Come," he said. Then Peter got down out of the boat, walked on the water and came toward Jesus. 30But when he saw the wind, he was afraid and, beginning to sink, cried out, "Lord, save me!" 31Immediately Jesus reached out his hand and caught him. "You of little faith," he said, "why did you doubt?" 32And when they climbed into the boat, the wind died down. 33Then those who were in the boat worshiped him, saying, "Truly you are the Son of God."2

Those of us who grew up in the church or have been Christians for a while have heard this story a *zillion* times. And we usually agree on the same takeaways. We talk about Peter's lack of faith that caused him to begin to sink when he took his eyes off of Jesus and started looking at his situation.

Sometimes, we'll talk about the fact that Peter was the only one who actually got out of the boat. I don't know why Peter didn't just say, "Lord, if it's you, come get in the boat." We'll never know this side of heaven what possessed Peter to ask Jesus to call him out onto the water. But for those of us brave enough to ask Jesus to call us out, we will undoubtedly be met with waves. However, God has a way of rewarding big faith if we keep our ears tuned to His voice.

It's incredible what Peter accomplished in this moment. And yes, he lost faith for a bit, but Jesus caught him—like He does us. Neither Peter's courage nor his lack of faith are really the point of this story. At least, I don't think so. In my mind, the point of this story is found in the last verse, which I skipped over for most of my life.

> [33]Then those who were in the boat worshipped him, saying, "Truly you are the Son of God."

It's about those still in the boat. Your risk-taking for the kingdom, empowered by the Holy Spirit, displayed in your communities, is what the world is waiting to see. Peter had faith enough for the risk. And yes, He partnered with Jesus in something incredible. But it wasn't for him. It was for those still in the boat. Peter's faith created a domino effect, stirring up a faith in the others that brought belief and worship. It works the same way with our risk-taking for the kingdom. As we listen for the voice of the Holy Spirit in our lives, calling us out onto the waves, we have an opportunity to partner with the Lord to live God-sized lives —lives worth following. But it's not for us. Our faith—this conviction that God is bigger than our circumstance and wants to do more in us and through us than we can ask or imagine—is always for others. We just happen to have the joy and privilege of partnering with Him in it.

Scott Harrison partnered with God and since charity: water began, they have funded 29,725 water projects for 8.4 million people around the world. Incredible! But it doesn't come easy.

There's a story in the Bible where four men are trying to get their paralyzed friend to Jesus.[3] They're carrying him on a stretcher of some kind, but they can't get to Jesus because the crowd is too large. What do these friends do? They climb onto the roof, dig through the clay tiles with their bare hands, and lower their friend down to Jesus because they know that if they can just get him to Jesus, their friend will be healed. The story says Jesus "saw their faith." Whether it's bringing people clean water, serving ice cream, or whatever it is God will ask you to do, Jesus wants to *see* our faith as we take risks for His kingdom. It likely won't come easy, but it will be worth it, and our faith will be evident by the dirt under our fingernails.

Chapter 12: Mystery

Growing up, all my wife ever wanted was to be a wife and a mom. She didn't have major career aspirations, she just wanted to care for her family. We've been married for almost two decades now and have two children. But raising kids has been very difficult for us—especially for my wife. Don't get me wrong, she's an amazing mother. But sometimes life doesn't turn out the way you imagine when you're growing up. Sometimes you feel like you can't win with your kids, and you wonder why everything feels so hard. Sometimes it's all you can do to get through the day, only to start up again in the same situation on the next. Our life isn't bad—not by any means. But it's challenging, and the natural tendency is to wonder if God maybe screwed up. Or if you missed something along the way.

Some of you still have no idea what God is calling you to. You feel like you've been pleading with Him for breakthrough, for clarity—and you have received neither.

My wife can relate. Maybe you're just trying to get through school, or working at what you feel is a dead-end job. Maybe you're successfully engaged in your workplace, but want God to use you for greater impact. I don't know where you are or what you're dealing with, but I will say this: God is good, and He is for you.

I once heard a pastor say, "God conceals matters *for* us, not *from* us." I think he's right. There's a kind of beauty and growth in the desert that you can't experience elsewhere. There's a breakthrough that is made sweeter through the seasons of contending.

My wife still hasn't been able to put her finger on that one thing that makes her excited to get out of bed, but I feel like she's circling around it. Part of it for sure is being an incredible mother and wife. There are lessons she's learning through the process that are bringing clarity. And she's blessing people along the way.

My wife is fiercely loyal. If you mess with her friends or family, she will cut you. But for those she cares about, she'll be the first one there if you need anything. She's open and honest and allows other people to be the same, especially moms who are having a tough time but don't feel like they can admit it. And while my wife still feels like she's searching for purpose, she both has it now, and is waiting for God to reveal it in greater detail.

God is mysterious, it's true. But I believe He still speaks and can make His plans known to us. He wants an intimate relationship with us. But on the other hand, He often doesn't answer—at least in the way we want and in the timing we hope for.

It's a tricky question we've all wrestled with. Truth is, we won't have a clear answer until heaven. But I've found some comfort in the fact that we do not worship an unknown God. There's a difference between the mysterious and the unknown. When something is mysterious, you have at least a sense of its presence. Something without that sense is just unknown. My wife is mysterious. I know her—I've spent years with her. But there's still much to discover. She continually surprises me. That's mystery—I know in part, but not in full.

Proverbs 25:2 says, "It is the glory of God to conceal a matter; to search out a matter is the glory of kings."[1] God is at times mysterious, but His desire is to be known. He uses mystery to encourage the hunt.

When I was in college, I started reading the stories of Sherlock Holmes by Sir Arthur Conan Doyle, which are great examples of mystery. The common theme with these stories, and any other mystery, is that the stories are driven by clues. There are clues hidden along the plot line that spark movement—whether to the answer or another clue. These clues are connected to the answer, and they have value because of that connection. The distinction between a mystery and the unknown is that, with the unknown, there is no starting point—no point of connection. It's like walking by hundreds of people on the streets of New York. You'll walk by them all without thinking about it because there is nothing to make you stop. But when you see someone you know, you pause and have a conversation. Without that seed of "knowing," however small it is, you've got nothing.

It's like my friend Greg experienced with his ice cream shop. He had a seed. Two words: "ice cream." But he didn't know what it would become. He was just obedient to walk towards the whisper. When his plans in Costa Rica fell through and he moved back to the States, he could have given up altogether, but he didn't.

Sometimes, it's God's mercy that He doesn't give us what we ask for. Thinking back on my life, I can come up with a handful of prayers that I am grateful God didn't answer. Maybe I wasn't ready for the thing I was praying for. Or maybe the thing I was praying for wasn't what I actually needed. Either way, God knew and had better plans for me than I knew at the time. Even though I was desperate for the answer I thought I needed, I didn't see a "Plan B." I didn't see any other door to walk through except the one I was trying to break down. But that verse in Proverbs 25 says our glory (which can be translated as "abundance" or "riches") is found in the seeking. So much of the time, the "praying without seeking" doesn't bring the answer to the prayer, as much as it aligns our hearts with His. We find our desires change, or we are able to rest in the fact that He's continually arranging the pieces of our lives to bring the solution that best advances His kingdom.

It is often said, hindsight is 20/20. Looking back, I've seen that what seemed like unanswered prayers weren't that at all. Rather, it was God, who knew what I was actually desiring in the deep places of my heart, working things together for good. But wow, doesn't it always seem to take longer than we'd like? Again, our riches and abundance are found in the seeking, and God is faithful to establish our steps.

Proverbs 16:9 says, "In their hearts humans plan their course, but the Lord establishes their steps."[2] Christians use it all the time. But it has greater significance than we realize. I've never known *exactly* what course to take. God bless those of you who knew exactly what you wanted and walked straight towards it. The weight of this verse still applies to you freaks, but for the rest of us, we often wander directionally towards our destination. Meaning, I know I don't want to head north, south, or west. So, I guess I'll walk east. But I'm not sure where exactly I'm headed—it could be Texas, Florida, or New York. Of course, I'm using direction figuratively. It could be that you know you don't want to work for someone or be a stay at home mom. Maybe you know you're creative and have a passion for making jewelry, so you walk in that direction and pray the

Lord establishes your steps along the journey. Or, maybe you're applying for a college that requires you to declare a major. You know you're not interested in engineering or agriculture, but you're curious about the human condition and why people do what they do, so you become a philosophy major, even though you're not sure about what the end goal is. These are just examples, and I hope you get the point. Most of us don't have a plan written out in exact detail, so we walk directionally into the fog, with the path becoming clearer as we continue.

But here's the thing about that word "establish" from Proverbs 16:9. When it says the Lord "establishes our steps," the word "establish" means, "to institute permanently by agreement."[3] Every step we take in obedience to the course we believe God has set us on, He makes permanent through our agreement and partnership with Him. He gives weight and purpose to each of our steps. You are never *just* anything when you do it for the kingdom of God. Your actions are being amplified by heaven. I don't take this verse to mean that He superimposes His will and robotically controls our paths. I believe this verse means that as we say "yes" to His lordship and kingdom, He says "yes" to us and makes each step—each of our decisions and actions—more impactful because He is in them. The Holy Spirt energizes and empowers the thing that we partner with God on. His plan was always to partner with us to see His kingdom on earth. When we are in agreement with His kingdom purposes, He establishes our steps. Even when we don't see the destination, if we are listening for and obeying the voice of the Holy Spirit, we can look back on our steps and see that God gave eternal impact to the path we walked.

So, keep contending. Keep searching. Never tire of seeking and knocking. Embrace the mystery and continue the hunt. Wake up early to pray and read the scriptures. Take every personality profile and strength assessment you can take. Surround yourself with mentors who can speak truth and hope into your life. Listen for the internal prompting of the

Holy Spirit. And when the Spirit speaks, listen and obey. As you find clarity in what God would have you do, make sure you do it with conviction and purpose—to create a city on a hill and bring the kingdom of God to earth.

Every vocation is sacred when it's co-opted by the kingdom! God will use your journey to draw you closer to Him, and you might just find that when you arrive at your destination, the destination was never the point at all. The journey, the building, and establishing with God is where the real treasure was found.

Chapter 13: Treehouses and Firm Foundations

We used to live in a home on two acres of land, so we had plenty of space. One summer, I decided to build my kids a treehouse in one of the big oak trees. They didn't spend much time outside, even though we had land enough for them to roam around on. My wife and I grew up on or near property, so living that way felt normal to us. We had a dog, chickens, and tons of space for the kids to explore. But they were totally content in their 10'x10' bedrooms, incessantly asking us to bring them water or food, or walk into their room to hand them that toy that's two feet away from them. My hope was that a treehouse would give them their own space outside, and would give us some small, but glorious, quiet time.

Problem with the treehouse was, I'm not very handy. Having me try to build a treehouse myself is ill-advised and will undoubtedly result in someone getting seriously injured. But, I decided to build it anyway.

I found a tree on our property shaped like a cobra about to strike. It was a great treehouse tree; I could literally walk up the trunk and into the treehouse. But because the tree was on a hillside, the front of the treehouse was going to be substantially higher off the ground than the back entryway of the treehouse from the tree trunk. There was about a 15-foot drop from the front of the treehouse to the ground, so I needed to support the front of the tree house with 20-foot 4"x4"s that went deep into the ground. Seriously dangerous. But there would be walls and stuff. What could go wrong, right?

After spending a day installing the 4"x4"s into the ground, I took a two month break. Those of you who have kids know how hard it is to get home improvement projects done. So, there it sat, just posts sticking out of the ground. But after my hiatus, I was on to the next task of bolting 2"x4"s around the posts, making a square which I would attach the floor joists to. I made quick work of that, and then took another break. This time, only one month. I was getting quicker each time I picked up a hammer!

Next was attaching the floor joists. Then I would install the floor, the walls, and the roof. Lastly, I'd slap a coat of paint on it, send the kids up, and see them again once high school graduation rolled around.

I couldn't get to the middle floor joists because the structure was too tall and my ladder was too short, so I decided to put a half sheet of plywood across the edges of the outside floor joists. If you can't picture this, just think....dangerous. Then, multiply said danger by 10.

As I lay on the plywood—15 feet up in the air—trying to screw in the last of the floor joists after months of working on this *stupid* treehouse, I found myself wanting to be done with the floor so I could move on to the walls and the paint. I was anxious to celebrate the accomplishment and start using the treehouse for the purpose for which it was being built. Lying there, hanging over the side, I had the all too common experience of trying to put the screws in the wood—one hand on the drill and one hand on the screw—only to have the drill slip and the screw fall to the ground before it caught the wood. I must have done this about 20 times. Grab my screwdriver, grab a screw. Hold the screw with one hand and the drill with the other. Press the screw to the wood, begin to drill....screw drops 15 feet to the ground. Repeat. Repeat. Repeat. The ground below the treehouse was starting to look like a minefield.

I also had a pencil behind my ear to mark where the hangers were supposed to go. In between dropping screws, I dropped the pencil. Every time something fell, I got up off my stomach, walked down the tree, down the hill, picked up the screw or pencil, walked back up the hill, up the tree, back onto my stomach—and began dropping stuff again. The final straw was when I accidentally knocked over my tape measure, which was resting on one of the joists. I lost it. Let me just say that the words coming out of my mouth were not blessings. As I was making my way down the tree for the twentieth time, I felt God reveal something so profound to me. It was one of those moments that you just know you'll never forget as long as you live.

He said, *"Spend your years on the foundation, not the walls."*

You see, I had been rushing the process, trying to get to the finished product, not realizing that the finished product is rarely the goal. Often, in God's upside-down kingdom, the process is the goal—the discovery, the journey—not the destination. Building the foundation is where the real treasure is found. The final product becomes sweeter and better for the journey. Are you rushing yourself? In the hustle and bustle of the day, do you forget the joy of your children? Your spouse? Your job? The sunshine? The day itself?

Even in Jesus' day, people were quick to forget what was most important. There's a story in the Bible about two sisters, Martha and Mary. Jesus and the disciples were passing through their village on the way to Jerusalem, so Mary and Martha invited them into their home. Martha started cooking a big meal to feed Jesus and the disciples, but Mary sat at Jesus' feet, listening to His teaching. Martha was so rushed, so distracted trying to get to what she thought was the goal—a big dinner that would satisfy the Savior—that she completely missed Him in the process. Martha, frustrated by her sister's laziness and unwillingness to help, approached Jesus, and—in classic sibling fashion— decided to tattle-tale.

"Lord, doesn't it seem unfair to you that my sister just sits here while I do all the work? Tell her to come and help me,"[1] she told Jesus.

But Jesus reminded her that she needs to spend her years on the foundation.

"My dear Martha, you are worried and upset over all these details! There is only one thing worth being concerned about. Mary has discovered it, and it will not be taken away from her."[2]

Martha didn't go wrong in wanting to cook Jesus dinner. It was an admirable goal. For Martha, this was simply a lesson in missing the point. Now, those of you who are more practical like my wife are going to say, "Well, *someone* had to make dinner. Mary wasn't going to do anything, so Martha started doing the real work by ministering to Jesus through His stomach."

But Jesus didn't challenge Martha because she was cooking. Earlier in verse 40, it says, "Martha was distracted by the big dinner she was preparing." Martha was *distracted*—that was the problem. Just like I was distracted by getting to the end of the treehouse project and not spending enough time making sure I had a firm foundation, Martha was so distracted by making this meal that she didn't spend enough time on the one thing she should have been concerned about, which was spending time at the feet of Jesus.

This foundational work is so important. Taking the time to make sure our "soil" is healthy and ready to grow what the Lord would wish to plant in our lives. Our foundation is built in times listening for the voice of the Lord, learning to hone our craft, learning to walk before we run. It's about not rushing through life and missing life in the process. Building a firm foundation requires that we be *present* in our lives— that our minds are quiet enough to hear the voice of the Spirit, that our hands are empty enough to carry what God would place in them, and that our bodies are healthy enough to do the work Jesus would call us to do. Before we get to the walls, we must build solid foundations. Even Jesus spent thirty years on his "foundation" before he went into a three-year ministry. Often, we want to spend three years training for a thirty-year ministry or occupation, and I wonder if Jesus might think we've got our priorities backwards. Maybe we're trying to build our walls too soon?

Now, I'm not sure what your walls are specifically, but it occurred to me that our walls are the things that people see. They are the outward manifestation of our inward desires. Our walls can be things like influence, beauty, security, or fame. They can be tangible as well. Your walls could be your job, your family, the side-project you've been hustling to get up and running, your wardrobe or bank account, your podcast or your non-profit. For me, my walls are writing a book, recording music, or speaking with the church.

I should say that I don't believe these "walls" are bad. Just the opposite, actually. I think we fail when we deny the authority and mantle the Lord has given each of us. We have to recognize we've been given a measure of "power." We all have talents and abilities that are unique, that should be fostered well and shared within the sphere of influence God has given us. Let's not get confused in the belief that pursuing the dreams God puts in us is selfish, or means we have bad motives. It's just that, like the story of Martha and Mary, we shouldn't be so distracted by our walls that we forget about our foundation. See, once you've got a solid foundation, the walls come up easy.

Remember Proverbs 16:9? The Lord "institutes our steps permanently by agreement." Our job is to make sure we've got a foundation in Him that is solid enough to support the life God wants us to live. Remember God created us to be a royal priesthood—a people to rule and reign with Him on earth. So, make sure you're well rooted!

Our problem isn't that our dreams are too big—it's often that they're too small. I don't know about you, but I don't want to look back on my life and see a story that didn't need God because it was too small.

But here's the thing. The quality of your foundation will determine the height of your structure. Take time on your foundation. Don't try to build walls higher than your foundation will support.

Have you ever played Jenga? As you pull wooden pieces from the bottom of the structure, you weaken the foundation and the tower begins to wobble. It's only a matter of time before it crumbles because the foundation can't support what you're building on top of it. Again, the quality of your foundation will determine the height of your walls.

In 1 Kings 6, Solomon begins building the temple of the Lord, to house the ark of the covenant. The stones used to build the foundation of the temple couldn't be cut at the temple site. They had to be prepared in the quarry by craftsmen and brought—finished—to the temple site. I won't go into the history of this requirement from Solomon, but it's a throwback to a command by God in Deuteronomy 27 not to use any iron tool on the stones of the altar on Mount Ebal. Can you imagine how much work this took?

Just to give you an idea of scale, the quarry (under Mount Moriah) is 330 feet wide and 650 feet deep. That's one football field wide and two football fields deep. Solomon hired 80,000 stonecutters and 70,000 carriers for the stones. No heavy machinery. They had to go into this quarry, cut the stones, and then haul them to the site of the temple.

Solomon didn't care how many people it took or how long it took. The stones used for the foundation of the temple had to be the best sourced and crafted he could find. It took him seven years to finish the temple. What amazes me is this: 1 Kings 6:18 says, "The inside of the temple was cedar, carved with gourds and open flowers. Everything was cedar; no stone was to be seen." Solomon used the finest materials and laborers he could find for a foundation that would never be seen.

What does it mean to focus on the foundation? It means instead of trying to figure out the end game, you just worry about the next play. It's not getting so focused on the closed door you're trying to beat down that you miss the six open doors around you. If Greg at Doc Burnstein's Ice Cream Lab would have focused on the walls, he would have given up long ago. But instead of trying to figure out how to achieve his dreams on his own, he set his attention on the Lord, and that foundation led to taller walls than Greg could have ever dreamt of building. If my pastor would have focused on the walls, he would have stayed put in Michigan where he had everything he thought he wanted. Instead, he surrendered to the lordship of Jesus and did the hard work of faith. My question for us is, are we willing to spend our years on the foundation? Are we willing to spend our time in the quarry, honing our craft, deepening our relationship with the Lord when we feel like we have more questions than answers?

My hope is that more of us experience this upwelling of dreams that can't be done outside of agreement and partnership with God. I don't want to build a life that didn't require Him. I want to live a God-sized life because I want God-sized healing and restoration for my community and for God's good world. How about you? I can't wait to see what kind of walls God builds through *your* obedience in building your foundation on the lordship of Jesus.

Chapter 14: Active Rest

Pagers, paper maps, land lines, and blockbuster video stores. All these things at one time were core to American culture, but are now obsolete. Why? Because they lost their purpose. They are no longer useful to society.

The plastic pink flamingo was created as a real solution to a real problem. It was made to distinguish homes, to set them apart against the monotony of the American suburb. But somewhere along the way, the pink flamingo lost its purpose and became a symbol of everything that's wrong with American culture. The same has happened to many Christians. We go to church on Sundays, we sing the songs and pray the prayers. We listen to worship music and (mostly) don't cuss. But something is missing. We feel a disconnect between the life we think we're supposed to live and the life we actually live. If you feel an aching in your bones telling you that this 60-hour work week, just-trying-to-hold-on kind of life can't be all there is, listen to the aching, because it's not. You were made for so much more.

God has given every human innate value by creating us in His image. Our purpose is to be set apart in order to bring real solutions to some of the biggest challenges facing our world. Featherstone's plastic flamingo didn't lose its value until it lost its purpose. How about you? Are you sitting on the bench, believing the lie that you don't have purpose? If so, you've got a decision to make. You can shrink into the lie, or grow into the truth that you have God-given value and purpose and are more loved than you could ever imagine. That this God who loves you wants to see you engage in His good world to bring healing and restoration in ways that only you can.

It's time to rediscover our purpose so that we can be a blessing to those around us and encourage others to do the same. Those who choose to take God at His word might not live the easiest life, but it will be one of purpose

and significance. But not through our own strength. If

you're feeling like you've got the weight of the world on

your shoulders and have to make all of this happen on

your own, take a deep breath. Relax and trust that it's God

who does the real heavy lifting in our lives. The people in

the stories I've shared worked hard, but because their

ventures were co-opted by the kingdom, God was the real

hero. We can, and are called to, simply abide in Christ—to

spend our time, not trying to make a name for ourselves

and build higher walls, but to sit at His feet and form a firm

foundation. He will take care of the rest.

In the fourth chapter, Matthew says, "But He (Jesus)

answered and said, "It is written, 'Man shall not live by

bread alone, but by every word (*rhema*) that proceeds out

of the mouth of God.""[1]

Rhema is a spoken word made by the *living* voice. It's the voice of the Holy Spirit—and it's what we should live on. His voice is what will give us peace, rest, and purpose. When you read the Bible, ask God for His *rhema* word—His voice that speaks straight to your heart.

As my relationship with my wife has deepened over the years, we've gotten to the point where we can finish each other's sentences. For those of you who are married, you may have the same experience. We're still very different, but we've developed a similar taste in food and movies and will sometimes even come out of our closets wearing scarily similar outfits. But it's not just my knowledge of my wife that makes our relationship different. It's that I've learned the intent of her heart. I don't just know *about* her, I *know* her. I know her character, what moves her, what angers her, what pleases her.

It's in the daily interactions with the Lord and His *rhema* word that we develop the same intimacy. I'm convinced that being busy is one of the greatest hindrances to deepening our relationships with the Lord. I understand modern life has put certain pressures on us, but we also make the bed we sleep in. It's as if Satan says, "If I can't kill them, I'll make them busy." There's a discipline to rest. It's something we haven't quite figured out yet. It's not that I'm unrealistic. I understand there are times when rest isn't possible. But it's critical we maintain "Sabbath" rest in our lives, even if at times it's just rest of spirit.

When things are moving at 100mph around us, we must take on what I call an "active rest." It's the intentional hard work of posturing our hearts towards calm in the storm. Like we talked about earlier, Jesus took a posture of rest in the storm. Did you know 75% of Americans sleep next to our phones, and 90% of us check our phones immediately upon waking? When it comes to rest, 40% of Americans sleep less than six hours per night[2] (down from nine hours per night in 1910). And as far as time spent online, 26% of American adults report they go online "almost constantly."[3] Vacations? About 37% of Americans take fewer than seven days of vacation per year. We *must* slow down.

But wait, you might be thinking. *Haven't you been telling us this whole time that we're supposed to rediscover our purpose, to hustle and do the hard work of faith in order to transform our communities?* Yes, but this cannot happen apart from the *rhema* word of God giving us life as we spend time in active rest. In the fourth chapter of Zechariah, the Lord says, "not by force, not by power, but by my Spirit."[4] The same principle applies to us. We're not going to transform anything. But God can! And He partners with us to do so. But we need time in active rest to separate the signal from the noise. This might mean you limit your time on your phone, or cancel your cable service, or take more days off this year. It *definitely* means that you soak in the scripture and in prayer—that you take time to listen for the *rhema* voice of the Holy Spirit. This kind of active rest is so critical for kingdom success. When I've experienced the voice of the Holy Spirit, it's usually in a whisper, not a shout. But if everything is shouting around you, hearing the whisper can be difficult. Maybe that's why Jesus so often went to a "quiet place to pray."

Common sense tells us that when the going gets tough, the tough get going, right? We hunker down, dig in our heels, and *make* a way forward. Sometimes, that's exactly what we need to do, but more frequently, we're called to pray and let God fight our battles for us.[5]

There's this great story in 2 Chronicles, chapter 20[6] that illustrates the power of worship and rest so beautifully. Here's the background. Jehoshaphat, the King of Judah has just heard there is an army marching toward them, intent on battle. What does King Jehoshaphat, a man of God, do to prepare his people for war? Well, he declares a fast, of course! I don't know about you, but if I were the king,

I'd probably make sure my people—and for sure my army—
were well fed. The last thing I'd want is a nation of "hangry"
people! But Jehoshaphat understands that the strength of
the Lord is stronger than the strength of men. He declares
a fast and calls all of Judah to gather together and seek
the help of the Lord. Upon the arrival of the people of
Judah and Jerusalem, King Jehoshaphat stands in front of
the assembly and, instead of sharing his military strategy
for the impending battle, he starts prophesying, foretelling
the truths of God and what He has done for them in
generations past. He says:

> [6]..."O Lord God of our fathers, are You not God
> in heaven...do You not rule over all the
> kingdoms of the nations...In Your hand is there
> not power and might, so that no one is able
> to withstand You? [7]Are You not our God, who
> drove out the inhabitants of this land before
> Your people Israel, and gave it to the
> descendants of Abraham Your friend

forever? ⁹'If disaster comes upon us—sword, judgment, pestilence, or famine—we will stand before this temple and in Your presence (for Your name is in this temple), and cry out to You in our affliction, and You will hear and save.'

Then, in one of the most beautiful declarations in the whole of the Bible, Jehoshaphat says:

¹²...we have no power against this great multitude that is coming against us; nor do we know what to do, but our eyes are upon You."

"But our eyes are upon You." That line gets me every time. Talk about taking a posture of rest and faith in the storm. Judah is about to go to war and by all human logic, thousands will likely die as they lose their land. The invading army is set *"to utterly kill and destroy them."* 7 And here is their king, wrestling with both truths—that they have no power against the multitude coming against them, but also, that God is powerful and willing to save. If we're honest, that's likely where we find ourselves much of the time. We look around and feel completely powerless and unprepared to deal with our situation, but we recognize that God is good, and He is able to work wonders in our lives. Sometimes, reminding ourselves of God's faithfulness in the past, as the people of Judah did, is the best offense we have in our lives.

Now back to the story. As all of Judah, women and children included, stand there asking the Lord for help, the Spirit of the Lord comes upon Jahaziel, and he begins to prophecy, foretelling what God will do for them.

> 15...Thus says the Lord to you: 'Do not be afraid
> nor dismayed because of this great
> multitude, for the battle is not yours, but

God's....[17]You will not need to fight in this battle. Position yourselves, stand still and see the salvation of the Lord, who is with you, O Judah and Jerusalem!' Do not fear or be dismayed; tomorrow go out against them, for the Lord is with you."

After hearing the word of the Lord, Jehoshaphat, King of Judah, bows his head with his face to the ground.

That's an important, but often overlooked, action from Jehoshaphat. It says he bowed his head with his face to the ground. According to the Greek historian Herodotus, there were regulations as to how two people of different social or military rank should greet one another. If I were to greet a person of equal rank, they would give me a kiss on the lips. If I were to greet someone of a slightly lower rank, they would give me a kiss on the cheek. If I were to greet someone of a very inferior social standing, custom would dictate that they would completely bow down to the person before them.

Jehoshaphat bowing before the Lord is an act of worship. But it's not just that he lowered himself before the Lord, acknowledging his inferior position. When we bow, we lower ourselves. But by lowering ourselves, we exalt the One we bow before. Like John the Baptist said, "He must increase, but I must decrease."[8]

After Jehoshaphat and the people of Judah acknowledge their submission to the Lord, the children start to party!

> [19]Then the Levites of the children of the Kohathites and of the children of the Korahites stood up to praise the Lord God of Israel **with voices loud and high**. *(emphasis added)*

The next morning, the people of Judah march out to the battlefield and Jehoshaphat makes another strange decision. He sends musicians out before the army! Now, I'm a musician, so I know firsthand how ridiculous this decision is. Trust me, you do *not* want me trying to protect you.

I'm not built for war. I'm built for skinny jeans and coffee shops. But there goes crazy 'ol Jehoshaphat again, sending the musicians out in front of the army with this song:

> 21..."Praise the Lord,
>
> For His mercy endures forever."

The mercy of God was their war cry. And, boy, did the Lord respond to their worship!

> 22Now when they began to sing and to praise, the Lord set ambushes against the people of Ammon, Moab, and Mount Seir, who had

come against Judah; and they were defeated.

Not one person from the invading army survived. And all the people of God did was worship! I say, "all they did," but the truth of the matter is that worship is the best offense we have. The people of Judah stood still in the middle of the storm, and they saw the prophecy fulfilled. Position yourselves, stand still, and see the salvation of the Lord who is with you.

Jehoshaphat and the people of Judah are great examples for us of what it means to rest on the truths of the Lord and wait on the *rhema* word of God. Their risk-taking created a situation for God to move in power. And we're still telling their story today.

We are called to form disciples and see the nations worship the one true God. But don't you think it's difficult for a nation to worship a God they've never experienced? We need more individuals, cities, states, and nations taking risks like the people of Judah. It's in our risk-taking and active rest that we see the glory of the Lord and experience His loving kindness and favor over our lives for the benefit of those around us. We've got two options: we can go at it alone, trying to make something happen on our own, or we can set our eyes on the Lord, follow the often unconventional voice of the Lord, and let Him fight the battles for us. It's not that I'm lazy. We've still got to show up to the battle. I just believe that living a God-sized life requires...well....God. Many of us have created very comfortable lives for ourselves. But we've all read stories of successful people who are still empty. They've got everything, but they're still unsatisfied. Maybe it's because we weren't made to be self-sufficient. We were made to live by every word that proceeds from the mouth of the Lord.[9]

So tomorrow, spend some time alone. Soak in the scripture and pray. Listen for the *rhema* word of God spoken by the Holy Spirit. Go to work with kingdom lenses on. Pray that God gives you opportunities to advance His kingdom. Don't weary of doing good, for at the proper time you will reap a harvest if you don't give up![10] Keep your attention on the Lord and your ear turned toward Heaven. God will handle the rest.

Chapter 15: Perspective

I have a daughter, which means I'm bound to look at all men suspiciously for the rest of my life. It also means I'm usually covered in glitter—my nemesis. I have no idea where the stuff comes from. But I've got a thought about glitter, which is this: glitter is like sin, easy to apply to your body, but *very* difficult to remove. Anyway...that's neither here nor there.

Having a daughter also means that, when she was younger, there were a handful of songs we would sing together on repeat. One such song is, "Twinkle, Twinkle, Little Star." This, in addition to "Jesus Loves Me," "Somewhere Over the Rainbow," and "Somewhere Out There" are on the list of our most frequently sung bedtime lullabies. One night as we were singing "Twinkle, Twinkle, Little Star," a thought occurred to me. In the span of the whole universe, our sun is only an average-sized star. It's 93 million miles away, burns at 27 million degrees Fahrenheit, and can fit

1.3 million Earths inside it.

"Twinkle, twinkle, little star?"

Perspective is everything. You wouldn't sing "Twinkle,

Twinkle" while standing in front of a supernova. It's the

same with our relationship to the Lord. Our distance to an

object determines our perspective, which dictates our

response. The more time we spend with the Lord, building a

firm foundation, the clearer (and more biblical) our

understanding and perspective will be about what He can

and wants to do with our lives.

Christian pastor and author A.W. Tozer said, "What comes

into our minds when we think about God is the most

important thing about us." This is important, not because of

the mental belief itself, but because our mental beliefs

have material implications. What I mean is that what we believe affects how we live.

In fact, what we believe can even change the biochemistry in our body! There's a study[1] I read about a woman who was suffering from extreme nausea and vomiting. Doctors who were testing the placebo effect on the human body offered the woman a "new, extremely potent" drug, telling her it would cure her nausea. A few minutes after taking the placebo, the woman's nausea was gone! More fascinating is that the placebo the doctors gave the woman was ipecac, a substance usually used to induce nausea! But there was something about the syrup being offered to her, along with the reassuring word of an authority figure, that triggered a biochemical response in her body, curing her symptoms. How much more do you think we can affect the symptoms of a sinful world if we believe the word of *the highest* authority!?

There've been a string of tragedies in the world lately, ranging from natural disasters to mass shootings. Perspective is more important than ever. In the rarely sung, final verse of one of my favorite hymns "Come Thou Fount,"[2] the author describes the future he looks forward to:

> *O that day when freed from sinning,*
>
> *I shall see Thy lovely face;*
>
> *Clothed then in the blood washed linen, How*
>
> *I'll sing Thy sovereign grace.*

But the reality is that Jesus has not yet come and made all things new. He has not wiped every tear from our eyes or done away with death, sorrow, crying, and pain.[3] We live in the tension between evil in the world and a good God. But our job as Christ-followers is to reconcile the world to the reality that God is good—to prophesy to the truth of the kingdom of God and to reveal the reality of that kingdom in our communities.

How can you help usher in this kingdom, even today? I've been saying it all along: you're never *just* anything when you're doing it for the kingdom. You are set apart, you are chosen, you are part of a royal priesthood. You were made to rule and reign with Jesus, and it can begin today!

Chapter 16: Regain Your Purpose

Okay, so let's wrap this up. You've got stuff to do.

Don Featherstone died in 2015 at the age of 79.

It has been said, "there are more plastic Featherstone flamingos in the world than real flamingos."[1] If there was ever a symbol for the pervasive, stale, lifeless Christianity that so many of us have come to know, it is what Don Featherstone's infamous plastic pink flamingo has become. Created to differentiate, to be set apart, but now known for its worst qualities. Remember, the plastic pink flamingo didn't lose its value until it lost its purpose. What was made to be a beautiful representation of the "real thing," became a lifeless caricature. Those who follow Jesus are empowered by the Holy Spirit to use our unique gifts to be a blessing to our communities and to our world. But too often, we're known as the antithesis of the God we worship: God is love, Christians are judgy; God is slow to anger, Christians are uptight and grumpy; God is a refuge, Christians won't welcome me in. I could go on, but you get the idea.

Please hear my heart on this. I'm not saying we need to be passive. There are sin issues in our world that need to be dealt with. The Bible says, "all have sinned and fallen short of the glory of God"[2]. But humans make bad judges, juries, and executioners. Let's spend our time in prayer and fasting, asking the Holy Spirit to do the work of conviction, both in ourselves and in those around us, as we echo the war cry of the Israelites: *"Praise the Lord, for His mercy endures forever!"*

It's time for the flamingo to be reborn—to regain the purpose for which it was created. You and I have to find a new way forward. We're not doing our generation any favors by living under the radar, with our goal to be "nice people." We're not doing the *next* generation any favors either. This new way forward won't come easy, and it won't leave us without scars. But I want my kids to see my scars, not to protect them from their own, but to show them they're not alone in their struggles. It's time to become the people Peter prophesied about in Acts 2:

> [17]"And it shall come to pass in the last days, says God, that I will pour out of My Spirit on all flesh; Your sons and your daughters shall prophesy, your young men shall see visions, your old men shall dream dreams. [18]And on my menservants and on My maidservants I will pour out My Spirit in those days; and they shall prophesy.[3]

I want my kids to see their dad taking big risks for the kingdom. I want to see people saved, healed, and restored. I want to see disciples made. I want the kingdom of Heaven to come to Earth.

I'm going to pray. I'm going to ask for miracles. I'm going to throw parties and invite the "wrong" people. I'm going to talk about how Jesus can change us. I'm going to rest and listen. I'm going to worship. I'm going to take risks and do the things God has asked me to do. You can do it, too—I believe in you!

But dependency on Jesus is necessary for deployment in the kingdom of God. So, where are you on your journey? Have you submitted to the lordship of Jesus? Are you being empowered by the Holy Spirit through listening and obeying? Are your gifts being utilized for the benefit of your community?

God only made one of you, so you're the only one who can do what you do. Don't take it for granted. Don't waste your time. Raise your kids, start your business, write your book, lead your church, record your album, repair your broken relationships, go to work with a new perspective, submit to the lordship of Jesus, spend time alone in the Word and in prayer. Take risks for the kingdom of God.

Regain your purpose, and go change the world!

Acknowledgements

Jenn, thank you for pushing me to get this book done despite the hurdles, long hours and worst possible time in our lives to try and write a book. I love you.

John Secunda, Chad Bohi and David Hutsko, you have been sounding boards, encouragers and examples of men who have taken big risks for the kingdom. Thank you for paving the way.

Notes

Flannel Board Theology

1. Matthew 28:18-20.

2. Luke 4:18-19.

3. 2 Corinthians 4:4 NIV.

4. C.S. Lewis, *Mere Christianity.* (London, Geoffrey Bles, 1952).

5. "Time Flies: U.S. Adults Now Spend Nearly Half a Day Interacting with Media," Nielsen.com, July 31, 2018, https://www.nielsen.com/us/en/insights/news/2018/time-flies-us-adults-now-spend-nearly-half-a-day-interacting-with-media.print.html.

6. Jeffrey M. Jones, "In U.S., 40% Get Less Than Recommended Amount of Sleep," Gallup.com, December 19, 2013, https://news.gallup.com/poll/166553/less-recommended-amount-sleep.aspx.

7. "Facts and Statistics," Anxiety and Depression Association of America, 2018, https://adaa.org/about-adaa/press-room/facts-statistics.

8. "Suicide Statistics," American Foundation for Suicide Prevention, 2019, https://afsp.org/about-suicide/suicide-statistics/.

9. "Youth Suicide Statistics," The Jason Foundation, 2019, http://prp.jasonfoundation.com/facts/youth-suicide-statistics/.

10. Romans 12:2.

Phoenicopteris Ruber Plasticus

1. "The Postwar Economy: 1945-1960," American History: From Revolution to Reconstruction and Beyond, 2012, http://www.let.rug.nl/usa/outlines/history-1994/postwar-america/the-postwar-economy-1945-1960.php.

2. "Levittown: The Archetype for Suburban Development." *American History Magazine*. October 2007.

3. "Changes in Women's Participation in the Labor Force in the 20th Century," Bureau of Labor Statistics, U.S. Department of Labor, February 16, 2000, https://www.bls.gov/opub/ted/2000/feb/wk3/art03.htm.

4. 1 Peter 2:9.

The Calling

1. "Wesleyan Quadrilateral." United Methodist Church, http://www.umc.org/what-we-believe/wesleyan-quadrilateral.

2. Psalm 139:13.

Slaves to Righteousness

1. Romans 1:1.

2. Romans 6:18.

3. Matthew 23:15.

4. Psalm 107:14.

5. 1 Corinthians 6:19-20.

6. Luke 22:42.

7. Luke 4:18.

Ruach

1. John 14:12 NKJV.

How We Listen

1. Numbers 22:28. (The bible is often a mirror to allow us to see ourselves in the story. If you're being a stinker, then God will use an ass to show you that you're being, well....you get it.)

Shepherd King

1. Revelation 3:12; 21:2, 10, 12, 16.

2. Matthew 6:10.

3. Matthew 5:14–16 NASB.

Those in the Boat

1. Matthew 14:22–24 NIV.

2. Matthew 14:25–33 NIV.

3. Luke 5:17–20.

Mystery

1. Proverbs 25:2 NIV.

2. Proverbs 16:9 NIV.

3. Merriam-Webster, "establish" (v.), https://www.merriam-webster.com/dictionary/establish

Treehouses and Firm Foundations

1. Luke 10:40.

2. Luke 10:41–42.

Active Rest

1. Matthew 4:4 NKJV.

2. Neil Howe, "America the Sleep Deprived," *Forbes.com*, August 18, 2017, https://www.forbes.com/sites/neilhowe/2017/08/18/america-the-sleep-deprived/#7e3a0461a385

3. Andrew Perrin and JingJing Jiang, "About a Quarter of U.S. Adults Say They Are 'Almost Constantly' Online," *PewResearch.org*, March 14, 2018, http://www.pewresearch.org/fact-tank/2018/03/14/about-a-quarter-of-americans-report-going-online-almost-constantly/

4. Zechariah 4:6 NIV.

5. Deuteronomy 3:22.

6. 2 Chronicles 20 NKJV.

7. 2 Chronicles 20:23 NKJV.

8. John 3:30 NKJV.

9. Deuteronomy 8:3.

10. Galatians 6:9.

Perspective

1. T.S. Sathyanarayana Rao, "The Biochemistry of Belief," Indian Journal of Psychiatry, Oct-Dec, 2009, 51(4): 239-41, https://www.ncbi.nlm.nih.gov/pmc/articles/PMC2802367/

2. Robert Robinson, "Come Thou Fount," 1757.

3. Revelation 21:4.

Regain Your Purpose

1. Bruce Zarozny, President and Owner, Cado Products. Cado Products purchased and owns the blow-mold inventory of Union Products.

2. Rom. 3:23 KJV.

3. Acts 2:17-21 NKJV.

Made in the USA
Las Vegas, NV
24 July 2023

75152059R00105